Character&Novelty CLOCKS & WATCHES

Identifications & Values

Jim & Merlyn Collings

COLLECTOR BOOKS
A Division of Schroeder Publishing Co., Inc.

Front cover: Magician Clock, $1,300.00 – 2,800.00; New Haven Character Watch Display, $2,200.00 – 3,600.00; Mickey Mouse Wristwatch, watch only, $500.00 – 800.00, hinged box only, $1,700.00 – 2,600.00; Popeye Alarm Clock, $800.00 – 3,200.00; Betty Boop Pocket Watch, $5,200.00 – 6,700.00.

Back cover: Dome-shaped Heartbeat Clock, $250.00 – 325.00; Shirley Temple Pocket Watch, $400.00 – 500.00; Statue of Liberty Clock, $200.00 – 450.00; Sally Rand Pendulette Clock, $375.00 – 475.00; Boy Scout Pocket Watch, $600.00 – 800.00; Admiral Dewey Pocket Watch, $700.00 – 1,200.00; Mandolin Player Alarm Clock, $700.00 – 1,200.00.

Cover design – Christen Byrd
Layout design – Lynda Smith

COLLECTOR BOOKS
P.O. Box 3009
Paducah, Kentucky 42002-3009

www.collectorbooks.com

Copyright © 2011 Jim and Merlyn Collings

The current values in this book should be used only as a guide. They are not intended to set prices, which vary from one section of the country to another. Auction prices as well as dealer prices vary greatly and are affected by condition as well as demand. Neither the authors nor the publisher assumes responsibility for any losses that might be incurred as a result of consulting this guide.

Proudly printed and bound in the
United States of America

Contents

Introduction

All the timepieces in this book are from our own private collection. We have a special interest in comic character and animated clocks. The hunt for these wonderful timepieces is an ongoing endeavor. It is almost like being a modern archaeologist.

We always thought the first cartoon-type timepiece was Mickey Mouse, until we discovered animated novelty items dating back to the nineteenth century. We are forever fascinated by the animation and movement that these clocks and timepieces have. It reminds one of owning a poor man's automaton. These relics of Americana are truly symbols of days gone by. These timepieces remind us of early radio shows, comic books, bubble gum cards, early TV shows, movie serials, scout meetings, premiums, and newspaper cartoon strips. The list of memories is endless.

These early timepieces are great conversational items. Their artwork, design, and in some cases, animation are unique. Most of these novel timepieces were very inexpensive. Consequently, they were thrown away, making them rare and scarce.

We have divided this book into 15 categories from advertising to miscellaneous. Included in the book are sections on new additions, trivia, and an index. We tried to alphabetize within each category wherever possible.

In addition to character and novelty timepieces we've included the following collectibles to accent some of the timepieces shown in the book. Some accent pieces are found in each category. For example, the Shirley Temple pocket watch is accented by her jewelry. The Dizzy Dean timepieces are shown with his jewelry and pin-backs. The Big Bad Wolf is accompanied by a match holder and bank. In the Scouting category we've included several Boy Scout fobs. We feel these accent pieces will enhance any timepiece collection. Hopefully, this will encourage future collectors to include some related items in their character and novelty timepiece collection.

We've tried to include current retail prices by developing a range based on the following factors: rarity, scarcity, aesthetic appeal, and overall condition. The elements of condition include: workability, case appearance, amount of fading, dial brightness, unblemished dial, and originality. Taking these elements into consideration the pricing ranges from least to highest, very good/fine, and very fine/excellent.

A timepiece with its original box would be valued separately. Its original box would have a value of equal or greater than the timepiece itself. Again, the value of the box would be based on scarcity, rarity, aesthetic appeal, overall condition, complete insert, and edge wear.

The pricing information is strictly our own opinion and not necessarily the opinion of our readers. It is based on 25 years of collecting timepieces, auction results, internet sales, toy shows, collector input, reference materials, and old advertising. None of these prices is etched in stone. We hope this pricing information will be beneficial in your quest for collectible timepieces. Hopefully, this book will be an invaluable reference guide.

Nothing in this book is for sale but we will entertain trades. We've tried to share our collection with our readers knowing there are probably many other timepieces and variations to be discovered.

Happy timepiece collecting.

Jim & Merlyn Collings

Buster Brown Pocket Watch
Date: c. 1908 • Maker: Ingersoll
Early comic Buster Brown pocket watch used to
advertise Blue Ribbon Shoes.
$200.00 – 400.00

Buster Brown Pocket Watch
Date: c. 1910 • Maker: Ingersoll
Variation used to advertise Buster Brown Shoes.
$200.00 – 400.00

Buster Brown Pocket Watch
Date: 1929 • Maker: Ansonia
Variation showing Buster Brown and Tige outside circle.
$200.00 – 400.00

Buster Brown Pocket Watch
Date: 1930s • Maker: Unknown
Scarce Buster Brown Pocket watch in color.
$300.00 – 500.00

Charlie Tuna Wristwatch
Date: 1971 • Maker: Star Kist Foods, Inc.
Watch sold as a premium.
$75.00 – 95.00

Charlie Tuna Wristwatch
Date: 1977 • Maker: Star Kist Foods, Inc.
Watch sold as a premium.
$75.00 – 95.00

Coca-Cola Pocket Watch
Date: 1948 • Maker: Ingersoll
Scarce and desirable, colorful.
$200.00 – 300.00

Coca-Cola Pocket Watch
Date: 1948 • Maker: Ingersoll
Coca-Cola decal on back of pocket watch.
$200.00 – 300.00

Coca-Cola Wristwatch
Date: 1957 • Maker: Tissot (Swiss)
Rare 17 jeweled watch with Coca-Cola button
attached to second hand. Month and date on dial.
$250.00 – $500.00

Dum Dum Pops Wristwatch
Date: 1970s • Maker: Lafayette Watch Co.
17 jeweled watch advertising lollipops.
$100.00 – 175.00

Funky Phantom Wristwatch
Date: 1970s • Maker: Unknown
Advertising cereal.
$45.00 – 65.00

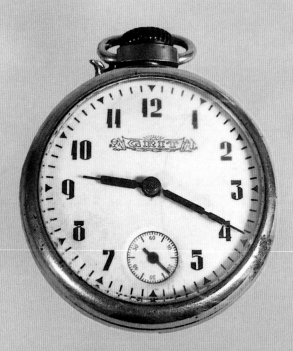

Grit Pocket Watch
Date:1930s • Maker: Unknown
Local advertising newspaper.
$75.00 – 125.00

Guinness Beer Pocket Watch
Date: c. 1930 • Maker: Ingersoll Ltd. (Great Britain)
Rare, "Guinness Time" in red letters,
animated colorful toucan pecking at beer
foam, smiling face on Guinness beer.
$500.00 – 700.00

Heinz Ketchup Wristwatch
Date: 1971 • Maker: Timex
Animated ketchup bottle on second hand
$75.00 – 150.00

Hershey Wristwatch
Date: 1970 • Maker: Lafayette Watch Co.
Hockey player moves with second hand.
$75.00 – 150.00

Indian Motorcycle Pocket Watch
Date: 1930s • Maker: Unknown
Scarce, Indian motorcycle pocket watch.
$150.00 – 250.00

Indian Fob
Date: 1930s • Maker: Unknown
Inscription reads "Old Indians Never Die."
$75.00 – 125.00

Indian Fob
Date: 1950s • Maker: Unknown
Inscription reads "Logan & Mystique Syracuse, N.Y."
$30.00 – 45.00

Ingersoll Dollar Pocket Watch in Box
Date: 1940s • Maker: Ingersoll
First pocket watch made in 1880s. Sold
for $1.00. Model shown here is The Yankee.
Pocket watch only $65.00 – 95.00
Box only $35.00 – 50.00

Kool-Aid Wristwatch
Date: 1970s • Maker: Premium (Swiss)
Attractive Premium watch.
$75.00 – 125.00

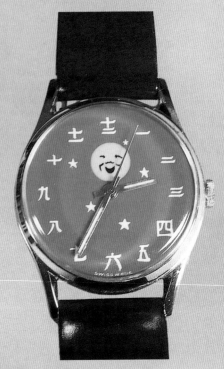

La Choy Soy Sauce Wristwatch
Date: 1970s • Maker: Premium (Swiss)
Watch numerals are Chinese characters.
$40.00 – 65.00

Mr. Peanut Wristwatch
Date: 1970 • Maker: Premium (Swiss)
Attractive Planters Peanut promotional watch.
$95.00 – 175.00

Numismatics Wristwatch
Date. 1976 • Maker: U.S. Mint
Bi-Centennial watch.
$75.00 – 135.00

Poll-Parrot Pocket Watch
Date: 1925 • Maker: Parrot Shoe Co.
Paul Parrot started this company. Small green parrot
shown on face of pocket watch.
$150.00 – 300.00

Poll-Parrot Fob
Date: 1925 • Maker: Parrot Shoe Co.
Greenish-yellow parrot is on fob.
$75.00 – 150.00

Poll-Parrot Fob
Date 1920s • Maker: Parrot Shoe Co.
Attractive parrot is in green, red, and yellow on fob.
$100.00 – 175.00

Poll-Parrot Wristwatch
Date: 1930s • Maker: Parrot Shoe Co.
Face of watch has words only.
Winder is at 1:00 position.
$100.00 – 200.00

Raid Wristwatch
Date: 1970s • Maker: Premium (Swiss)
Mosquito revolves on disc as second hand. 17 jeweled.
$75.00 – 150.00

Red Goose Pocket Watch
Date: c.1920s • Maker: Unknown
Red Goose advertises "School Shoes" (paper face).
$150.00 – 300.00

Red Goose Pocket Watch
Date: 1927 • Maker: Unknown
Scarce, "Friedman Shelby All Leather
Shoes" painted on tin face.
$300.00 – 700.00

Red Goose Wristwatch
Date: 1927 • Maker: Unknown
Scarce, painted tin face. Winder at 1:00 position.
$300.00 – 700.00

Red Goose Pin
Date: 1920s • Maker: Unknown
Painted wooden pin, possibly a give-away.
$25.00 – 75.00

Ritz Pocket Watch
Date: 1950s • Maker: National Biscuit Co.
Promotional pocket watch. Ritz crackers used in place
of numbers for hours.
$100.00 – 250.00

Ritz Bag
Date: 1950s • Maker: National Biscuit Co.
Original sample bag for a Ritz cracker.
Came with pocket watch.
$25.00 – 75.00

Ritz Wristwatch
Date: 1971 • Maker: National Biscuit Co.
Scarce, highly desirable promotional watch.
$150.00 – 300.00

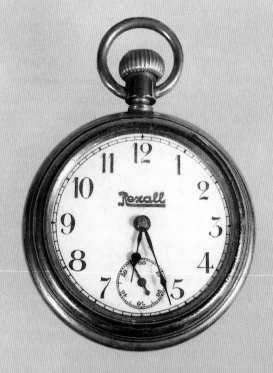

Rexall Pocket Watch
Date: 1930s • Maker: Unknown
Rexall Drug Store promotional pocket watch.
$75.00 – 175.00

Robin Hood Shoes Pocket Watch
Date: 1929 • Maker: New Haven
Outline of Robin Hood in gold, also numbers.
$150.00 – 275.00

Robin Hood Shoes Premium
Date: 1930s • Maker: Made in Japan
Mechanical premium "None So Good As."
$25.00 – 75.00

Sesqui-Centennial Pocket Watch
Date: 1926 • Maker: Ansonia Clock Co.
Celebrates 150th year of American Independence.
$200.00 – 400.00

7-Up Wristwatch
Date: 1970s • Maker: Promotional (Hong Kong)
Colorful with 7-Up trademark.
$50.00 – 90.00

Tommy Ticker Pocket Watch
Date: 1920s • Maker: New Haven
Pocket watch in box "True Time Tellers."
Pocket watch only $75.00 – 125.00
Box only $75.00 – 100.00

Tommy Ticker Wristwatch
Date: 1920s • Maker: New Haven
Wristwatch in box, "True Time Tellers."
Winder is at 1:00 position.
Wristwatch only $75.00 – 125.00
Box only $75.00 – 100.00

Twinkies Happy Shoes Wristwatch
Date: 1926 • Maker: New Haven
"Happy Shoes for Busy Feet." Winder is at 1:00 position.
$100.00 – 200.00

Advertising

United Airlines Wristwatch
Date: 1970s • Maker: Promotional
"We Are United" on dial.
$40.00 – 75.00

USA Airlines Wristwatch
Date: 1985 • Maker: Avion (Hong Kong)
Map of USA with unusual bubble top.
$40.00 – 75.00

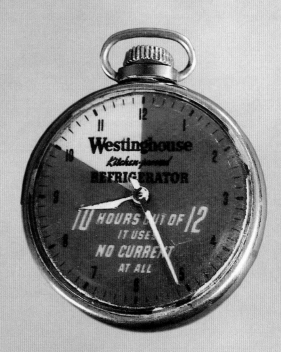

Westinghouse Pocket Watch
Date: 1950s • Maker: Promotional
Pocket watch in box. Emphasized Westinghouse refrigerator as an energy saver.
Pocket watch only $75.00 – 150.00
Box only $75.00 – 100.00

Westinghouse Pocket Watch
Date: 1950s • Maker: Promotional
Face is red and yellow. Advertises being an energy saver for Westinghouse refrigerator.
$100.00 – 200.00

Alarm Clock Types

Bell Tower Clock
Date: c. 1933 • Maker: Lux Clock Co.
Small animated bell in church tower. Clock in blue
picture frame setting, also came in white frame.
$125.00 – 225.00

Blacksmith Elf Clock
Date: 1930s • Maker: Germany
Elf has animated arm. Possible hand-painted dial.
$250.00 – 450.00

Blacksmith Clock
Date: 1950s • Maker: Paico
Large round clock with blacksmith moving arm.
$125.00 – 200.00

Bull Fighter Clock
Date: 1890s • Maker: Germany
Charging bull moves head.
$400.00 – 800.00

Drum Major Clock
Date: 1930s • Maker: Germany
Left arm holding baton is animated.
$250.00 – 450.00

Drunk Clock
Date: 1880s • Maker: Unknown
Drunk lying down in forest moves arm
and umbrella. Deer is watching him.
Clock rests on fancy cast-iron base.
$300.00 – 500.00

Grist Mill Clock
Date: 1930s • Maker: Germany
Grist mill water wheel turns.
Price: $250.00 – 450.00

"Happy Days" Clock
Date: 1933 • Maker: Lux Clock Co.
Emphasizes repeal of prohibition. Man's arm with beer
mug moves up and down.
$150.00 – 250.00

Hopalong Cassidy Clock
Date: 1950 • Maker: U.S. Time
No alarm, black enamel case.
$175.00 – 375.00

Ingersoll Catalin Alarm Clocks
Date: 1948 • Maker: Ingersoll
Both clocks have alarms.
Came in an assortment of colors.
$75.00 – 175.00 each

Landscape Clock
Date: 1930 • Maker: Lux Manufacturing Co.
Country scene with alarm.
$125.00 – 175.00

Landscape or Pastoral Clock
Date: 1950s • Maker: Lux Manufacturing Co.
Country scene with alarm.
$95.00 – 145.00

Maltese Falcon Clock
Date: 1991 • Maker: Turner Ent.
Alarm clock showing Humphey Bogart and Mary Astor.
Celebrating 50th anniversary of this famous movie.
$75.00 – 125.00

Mickey Mouse Electric Clock
Date: 1933 • Maker: Ingersoll
Scarce Mickey Mouse makes complete revolution. Disney characters appear on top and sides. Being electric could be hazardous to children.
$600.00 – 900.00

Mickey Mouse Clock
Date: 1933 • Maker: Ingersoll
Scarce. Three little Mickey images move at the 6:00 position. Popular clock with wind-up mechanism, company forgot alarm mechanism.
$500.00 – 800.00

Mickey Mouse Clock
Date: 1933 • Maker: Ingersoll
Scarce. Five Disney characters are shown on top and sides of wind-up clock.
$500.00 – 800.00

Mickey Mouse Clock
Date: 1933 • Maker: Ingersoll Ltd.
Scarce. English wind-up version. Has two
moving Mickey images at 6:00 position.
Porcelain face, yellow shorts, gloves, and shoes.
$600.00 – 900.00

Mickey Mouse Alarm Clock
Date: 1947 • Maker: Ingersoll
First Mickey Mouse alarm made since 1934.
Clock only $175.00 – 225.00
Box only $175.00 – 275.00

Mickey Mouse Catalin Alarm Clock
Date: 1949 • Maker: Ingersoll/U.S. Time
Mickey's arms and hands act as hour and minute hands.
$200.00 – 300.00

Monkey Shaving Barber Clock
Date: c. 1915 • Maker: Germany
No alarm. Clock on metal swivel
stand. Humorous theme.
$400.00 – 800.00

Pharmacist or Druggist Clock
Date: 1878 • Maker: Waterbury Clock Co.
Rare, no alarm. Pharmacist moves
arm while using pestle.
$800.00 – 1,200.00

Popeye Alarm Clock
Date: 1935 • Maker: New Haven
Rarest comic character alarm clock.
Showing several members of Thimble Theater on
side, back, and bottom. Popeye's arms and
hands act as hour and minute hands.
$800.00 – 3,200.00

Popeye Alarm Clock
Date: 1935 • Maker: New Haven
Rare colorful decals adorn this rare clock.
$800.00 – 3,200.00

Shoeshine Boy Clock
Date: 1930s • Maker: Lux Clock Co.
No alarm. Animated clock showing
boy shining lady's shoes.
$225.00 – 400.00

Shoeshine Boy Clock
Date: 1960s • Maker: Lux Clock Co.
Same as earlier version only larger clock.
$100.00 – 175.00

Teacher Clock
Date: 1880s • Maker: Germany
No alarm. Animation shows teacher
hitting pupil with hickory stick.
$600.00 – 900.00

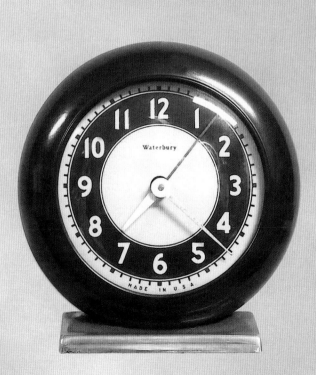

Waterbury Alarm Clock
Date: 1946 • Maker: Waterbury
Decorator clock. Came in an assortment of colors.
$75.00 – 150.00

"Way Down South" Alarm Clock
Date: 1938 • Maker: Westclox
Depicts two black children sitting on chairs.
$200.00 – 300.00

Windmill Clock
Date: 1930s • Maker: Germany
No alarm. Possibly hand-painted face. Windmill
is animated and has decorative frame.
$175.00 – 275.00

Windmill Clock
Date: 1950s • Maker: Holland
No alarm. Animated windmill.
$75.00 – 150.00

Windmill Clock
Date: 1940s • Maker: Holland
No alarm. Hand-painted tin face. Animated windmill.
$100.00 – 175.00

Windmill Clock
Date: 1930s • Maker: Germany
No alarm. Animated windmill.
$75.00 – 125.00

Animated Alarm Clocks

Animated Mouth Alarm Clock
Date: 1887 • Maker: New Haven
Rare. Girl's mouth moves as clock ticks away.
$800.00 – 1,200.00

Aristocats Alarm Clock
Date: 1977 • Maker: Bayard (France)
Mother's head rocks back and forth.
$125.00 – 200.00

Ballerina Alarm Clock
Date: 1960s • Maker: Rensie Watch Co. (Germany)
Unique clock with dancing ballerina, alarm,
and music box. Case is flowered black enamel.
Alarm works with music or bell sound.
$150.00 – 225.00

Ballerina Alarm Clock
Date: 1960s • Maker: Landau (Germany)
Radio style case with music and
dancing ballerina as alarm.
$100.00 – 175.00

Ballerina Alarm Clock
Date: 1950s • Maker: Germany
Thoren's Swiss movement, plays *Tales of Vienna
Woods* as ballerina dances inside dome.
$100.00 – 175.00

Babar Alarm Clock
Date: 1971 • Maker: Bayard (France)
Elephant's head moves up and down.
$125.00 – 200.00

Bambi Alarm Clock
Date: 1972 • Maker: Bayard (France)
Butterfly moves on Bambi's tail.
$150.00 – 250.00

Bayard Alarm Clock Box
Date: 1970s • Maker: Bayard (France)
Photo shows later box,
earlier boxes were quite decorative.
$50.00 – 75.00

Bayard Alarm Clock
Date: 1920s • Maker: Bayard (France)
Scarce. Balance wheel is shown at 6:00 position.
Marine time is indicated on face of clock.
Back of clock has engraved lion.
$300.00 – 500.00

Bear Alarm Clock
Date: 1970s • Maker: Bayard (France)
Friendly bear has moving head.
$125.00 – 175.00

Big Bad Wolf Alarm Clock
Date: 1934 • Maker: Ingersoll
Wolf opens and closes his mouth, three pigs are
shown on dial as well. Animated arms act as hour
and minute. Writing on face of clock reads
"Who's Afraid of the Big Bad Wolf?"
$400.00 – 800.00

Black Boy Alarm Clock
Date: 1915 • Maker: K.C. Co. (Wurtenburg, Germany)
Scarce. Eyes roll from side to side.
$500.00 – 800.00

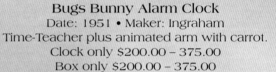

Bradley Time (Mickey Mouse) Alarm Clocks
Date: 1983 • Maker: Bradley
Mickey on left has animated feet. Mickey
on right has animated head.
Clock only $75.00 – 125.00 each
Clock in box $100.00 – 150.00 each

Bugs Bunny Alarm Clock
Date: 1951 • Maker: Ingraham
Time-Teacher plus animated arm with carrot.
Clock only $200.00 – 375.00
Box only $200.00 – 375.00

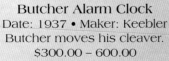

Butcher Alarm Clock
Date: 1937 • Maker: Keebler
Butcher moves his cleaver.
$300.00 – 600.00

Charlie McCarthy Alarm Clock
Date: 1938 • Maker: Gilbert
Rare. Charlie's mouth opens like a
vent doll. Also comes in round case.
$900.00 – 2,200.00

Charlie McCarthy Alarm Clock
Date: 1938 • Maker: Gilbert
Rare. Usually found in silver or red case.
$900.00 – 2,200.00

Chicken Pecking Alarm Clock
Date: 1968 • Maker: Smiths (Great Britain)
Animated chicken pecking in farmyard.
$75.00 – $150.00

Cobbler Alarm Clock
Date: 1880s • Maker: Germany
Animated apprentice shining boot.
$500.00 – 800.00

Cobblers Alarm Clock
Date: 1920s • Maker: Germany
Double animation. Cobbler and
apprentice both move hands.
$400.00 – 700.00

Cowboy Alarm Clock
Date: 1950s • Maker: Smith Alarm (Great Britain)
Cowboy rocks on horse.
$125.00 – 225.00

Cowboy Alarm Clock
Date: 1960s • Maker: Peter (Germany)
Horse and rider rock back and forth at 4:00 position.
$60.00 – 100.00

Dancing Mickey and Minnie Alarm Clock
Date: 1933 • Maker: Ingersoll
Rare. Possible prototype, "W.E.D. Prod." on dial. Animated Mickey and Minnie dancing. Notice long-billed Donald
and Horace Horsecollar shown on face as well.
$700.00 – 1,500.00

Donald Duck Alarm Clock
Date: 1950 • Maker: Glen Clock (Scotland)
Scarce. Donald Duck moves head back and forth.
$400.00 – 600.00

Donald Duck Alarm Clock
Date: 1964 • Maker: Bayard (France)
Donald's head rocks back and forth.
$150.00 – 300.00

Donkey Alarm Clock
Date: 1950s • Maker: Jaz (France)
Over-sized, donkey moves head as he pulls
carriage. Printed on face is "Peau D' Ane."
$250.00 – 350.00

Donkey and Boy Alarm Clock
Date: 1890s • Maker: Jungham (Germany)
Rare. Over-sized clock with double animation. Boy
moves stick hitting kicking mule.
$900.00 – 1,800.00

Early Bird Alarm Clock
Date: 1935 • Maker: U.S.A.
Variation 1, animated bird capturing a worm.
$175.00 – 225.00

Early Bird Alarm Clock
Date: 1946 • Maker: Westclox (Canada)
Variation 2, slightly different scene on dial.
$150.00 – 200.00

Gamblers Alarm Clock
Date: 1890 • Maker: Junghans
Rare. Double aniamtion. Gambler moves arm as he
thows dice. Dice disappear as second movement.
$800.00 – 1,500.00

Hey Diddle Diddle Alarm Clock
Date: 1920s • Maker: Smith Alarm (Great Britian)
Small doggie moves head at 7:00 position.
$125.00 – 200.00

Howdy Doody Alarm Clock
Date: 1950s • Maker: Kagran
Rare. "Clock-A-Doodle" tin litho. Double movement,
Howdy swings as pendulum and Flub-a-Dub pecks at
bird feeder. Bell rings every 15 seconds.
Without tree stand, $800.00 – 1,400.00
With tree stand (not shown), $1,500.00 – 3,400.00

Howdy Doody Alarm Clock
Date: 1950s • Maker: Kagran
Rare. "Clock-A-Doodle" tin litho. Rear view showing
Clarabelle, Princess Winter-Spring-Summer-Fall,
and Mr. Bluster shown on sides of house.
$800.00 – 1,400.00

Magic Castle Alarm Clock
Date: 1979 • Maker: Bradley
Disney characters move out of castle into
tent while music plays. White case.
$100.00 – 200.00

Magic Castle Alarm Clock
Date: 1979 • Maker: Bradley
Same as above. Case is red.
$100.00 – 200.00

Magic Castle Alarm Clock Box
Date: 1979 • Maker: Bradley
Mickey Mouse animated Disney
musical alarm clock box.
$20.00 – 35.00

Mandolin Player Alarm Clock
Date: 1887 • Maker: New Haven
Rare. Player strums on mandolin.
$700.00 – 1,200.00

Mickey Mouse Alarm Clock
Date: 1934 • Maker: Ingersoll
Scarce. First Mickey Mouse Disney clock
with an alarm. Moving head. Red version shown.
$350.00 – 750.00

Mickey Mouse Alarm Clock
Date: 1934 • Maker: Ingersoll
Scarce. Wagging-head Mickey.
Uncommon green version shown.
$400.00 – 800.00

Mickey Mouse Alarm Clock
Date: 1964 • Maker: Bayard (France)
Mickey's head moves back and forth.
$175.00 – 275.00

Monkey Shaving Barber Alarm Clock
Date: 1920s • Maker: Germany
Animation shows monkey shaving barber. Clock is
called "tin can" or "long-legged" clock. One alarm.
$200.00 – 350.00

Monkey Shaving Barber Alarm Clock
Date: 1920s • Maker: Germany
Triple alarm.
$250.00 – 400.00

Mountie Alarm Clock
Date: 1950s • Maker: Ingraham (Canada)
Canadian Mountie rocks on horse near Indian village.
$150.00 – 250.00

Noddy and Big Ears Alarm Clock
Date: 1950s • Maker: Smiths (Great Britain)
Very colorful with Noddy moving head.
$100.00 – 185.00

Olympian Alarm Clock
Date: 1920s • Maker: Germany
Rare. Olympian moves and does
somersaults on parallel bar.
$800.00 – 1,400.00

Organ Grinder and Monkey Alarm Clock
Date: 1920s • Maker: Lux (Waterbury)
Organ grinder turns handle on hurdy-gurdy.
$400.00 – 675.00

Organ Grinder and Bear Alarm Clock
Date: 1930s • Maker: Lux (Waterbury)
Organ grinder turns handle on hurdy-gurdy.
$350.00 – 575.00

Owl Alarm Clock
Date: 1960s • Maker: Smiths (Great Britain)
Owl's eyes move sideways.
$85.00 – 165.00

Peanut Roaster Vendor Alarm Clock
Date: 1930s • Maker: Lux (Waterbury)
Black boy turns handle as peanuts roast.
$450.00 – 750.00

Pecos Bill Alarm Clock
Date: 1971 • Maker: Bayard (France)
Disney character with moving arm and head.
$125.00 – 200.00

Pinocchio Alarm Clock
Date: 1967 • Maker: Bayard (France)
Jiminy Cricket moves head at 12:00 position.
Pinocchio characters adorn face of clock.
$150.00 – 300.00

Pixie Alarm Clock
Date: 1950s • Maker: Bingo (U.S.A.)
Pixies on moving see-saw.
$125.00 – 200.00

Pluto Alarm Clock
Date: 1964 • Maker: Bayard (France)
Disney's Pluto has animated head.
$175.00 – 275.00

Policeman Alarm Clock
Date: c. 1915 • Maker: Germany
Scarce. Policeman moves hand to stop traffic for little
dog crossing the street. Clock case is made of wood.
$600.00 – 1,100.00

Pools Alarm Clock
Date: 1950s • Maker: Smith Alarm (Great Britain)
Double animation. Man is moving pencil in hand. Wom-
an is reading moving numbers showing soccer results.
$350.00 – 500.00

Popeye Alarm Clock
Date: 1968 • Maker: Smiths (Great Britain)
Swee'pea is moving head at 7:00 position.
$150.00 – 250.00

Pumpkin Head or Mustache Man Alarm Clock
Date: 1960s • Maker: Bayard (France)
Head and mustache
moving at 12:00 position.
$100.00 – 175.00

Roy Rogers Alarm Clock
Date: 1951 • Maker: Ingraham
Roy and Trigger animated at 5:00 position.
Background is a desert scene with a gold-toned bezel.
Clock only $150.00 – 300.00
Box only $75.00 – 150.00

Roy Rogers Alarm Clock
Date: 1951 • Maker: Ingraham
Roy Rogers and Trigger moving at 5:00
position with desert scene background.
Bezel is sky blue picture frame.
$175.00 – 325.00

Showboat Alarm Clock
Date: 1956 • Maker: Lux (Waterbury)
Animated paddle wheel.
$125.00 – 200.00

Showboat Alarm Clock
Date: 1970s • Maker: Lux (Robertshaw)
Animated paddle wheel. Sealed in box.
$75.00 – 150.00

Snow White Alarm Clock
Date: 1960s • Maker: Bayard (France)
Disney Snow White characters adorn the face
of clock. Bluebird moves at 12:00 position.
$150.00 – 300.00

Soccer Alarm Clock
Date: 1960s • Maker: Peter (Germany)
Animated leg of soccer player.
$75.00 – 125.00

Spinning Wheel Alarm Clock
Date: 1950s • Maker: Lux (Waterbury)
Animated spinning wheel.
$125.00 – 200.00

Spinning Wheel Alarm Clock
Date: 1950s • Maker: Lux (Waterbury)
Double animation. Spinning
wheel and treadle both move.
$175.00 – 275.00

Sylvester Alarm Clock
Date: 1974 • Maker: Bayard (France)
Warner Bros. characters. Tweety Bird
moves above Sylvester's head.
$150.00 – 225.00

Teacher Alarm Clock
Date: 1950s • Maker: Smith Alarm (Great Britain)
Double animation. Teacher moves pointer
as numbers change on chalkboard.
$350.00 – 500.00

Trafalgar Square Alarm Clock
Date: 1950s • Maker: Smith Alarm (Great Britain)
Animated pigeon at 7:00 position.
$200.00 – 300.00

Trapeze Man Alarm Clock
Date: 1890s • Maker: Junghans (Germany)
Rare. Trapeze man swings back and forth
and does somersaults, brass case.
$900.00 – 1,700.00

Trapeze Man Alarm Clock
Date: 1890s • Maker: Junghans (Germany)
Rare. Trapeze man swings back and forth
and does somersaults. Copper case.
$900.00 – 1,700.00

Trout Fisherman Alarm Clock
Date: 1950s • Maker: Ingraham
Hooked trout jumping out of water.
$300.00 – 450.00

Waterwheel or Grist Mill Alarm Clock
Date: 1950s • Maker: Lux (Waterbury)
Scarce. Animated water wheel.
$275.00 – 400.00

Westerner Alarm Clock
Date: 1950s • Maker: Ingraham (Canada)
Scarce. Canadian version of Roy Rogers
and Trigger. Animation at 5:00 position.
$275.00 – 400.00

Woody Woodpecker Alarm Clock
Date: 1959 • Maker: Columbia Time
Variation 1. Animated Woody at Woody's Cafe.
Glow-in-the-dark hands and numbers.
$150.00 – 275.00

Woody Woodpecker Alarm Clock
Date: 1960s • Maker: Hong Kong
Variation 2. Alarm located in tree hole.
Animated Woody at 6:00 position.
Clock only $125.00 – 250.00
Box only $100.00 – 200.00

Woody Woodpecker Alarm Clock
Date: 1960s • Maker: Westclox (Hong Kong)
Variation 3. Clock face is lighter in color. Clouds are
added to scene. Westclox is printed on face. Blue case.
$150.00 – 275.00

Category 4
Animated Shelf Clocks

Aquarium Clock
Date: 1950s • Maker: United Clock Co.
Revolving cylinder shows fish swimming
below ship's wheel. Electric with light.
$200.00 – 400.00

Aquarium Clock
Date: 1950s • Maker: Sessions
Angel fish move with hands of clock.
Aquarium lights up electrically near 6:00 position.
$175.00 – 300.00

Ballerina Clock
Date: 1940s • Maker: United Clock Co.
Ballerina turns while music plays. Ballerina
and clock are connected in wooden case.
Ballerina's dome lights up.
$175.00 – 300.00

Ballerina Clock
Date: 1950s • Maker: United Clock Co.
Scarce. Dancing ballerina and clock are not
connected. Early plastic case. Electrically lit dome.
$200.00 – 400.00

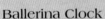

Bartender Clock
Date: c. 1933 • Maker: United Clock Co.
Clock case resembles cathedral radio.
Bartender moves arm while mixing drink. Made
after repeal of Prohibition. Non-electric.
$200.00 – 400.00

Blacksmith Clock
Date: 1950s • Maker: Mastercrafters
Fire lights up as blacksmith moves arm.
Electric movement.
$125.00 – 200.00

Boy and Girl on Swing Clock
Date: 1940s • Maker: United Clock Co.
Electric movement that lights up. Animation shows boy
and girl swinging. Desirable early green plastic case.
$150.00 – 225.00

Boy and Girl on Swing Clock
Date: 1950s • Maker: United Clock Co.
Animation shows boy and girl swinging.
Lights up electrically. Maroon colored case.
$125.00 – 200.00

Church Bell Ringer Clock
Date: 1950s • Maker: Mastercrafters
Church bell moves as bell ringer pulls on rope.
Interior of church lights up, works electrically.
$175.00 – 300.00

Columbus Clock
Date: 1908 • Maker: Western Clock Mfg. Co.
Bronze-plated cast-iron decorative clock. Souvenir
originally ordered for the Columbian Exposition of
1892 – 1893. Columbus, Indians, and ship are
embossed on clock. Wind-up clock, not animated.
$150.00 – 300.00

Covered Wagon Clock
Date: 1950s • Maker: United Clock Co.
Covered wagon lights up.
Animated driver moving horse whip.
$200.00 – 300.00

Cowboy Clock
Date: 1950s • Maker: United Clock Co.
Cowboy moves lasso electrically.
$125.00 – 225.00

Cowboy and Horse Clock
Date: 1950s • Maker: United Clock Co.
Cowboy moves lasso. Clock is electric.
$150.00 – 250.00

Dancers Clock
Date: 1950s • Maker: United Clock Co.
Four Victorian couples dance in a ballroom.
Covered by a glass case. Electric.
$175.00 – 250.00

Davy Crockett Clock
Date: 1954 • Maker: Haddon
Scarce. Davy on bucking horse move as they
encounter a bear. Pressed wood with handsome
dioramic scene. Creek Indian Wars, Congress, and
The Alamo are painted in black on the viewing window.
$500.00 – 850.00

Davy Crockett Clock
Date: c. 1948 • Maker: United Clock Co.
Scarce. Variation 1. Statue of Davy and
Indian adorn spelter metal case. Bottom lights
up as Davy observes. Revolving cylinder
shows Indians moving around covered wagon.
$375.00 – 575.00

Davy Crockett Clock
Date: c. 1948 • Maker: United Clock Co.
Variation 2. Spelter metal case adorned with Davy
and Indian. No animation. Diorama scene lights
up to reveal bear in woods with Davy observing.
$175.00 – 275.00

Farm Clock
Date: 1940s • Maker: United Clock Co.
Case is made of spelter metal. Colonial type farm
scene. Thermometer is attached to silo. Wind-up
animation depicts colonial drummer moving his arm.
$275.00 – 375.00

F.D.R. "Man of the Hour" Clock
Date: 1933 • Maker: United Clock Co.
Franklin D. Roosevelt trying to steer the nation
with the New Deal. Clock is electric, no animation.
$75.00 – 150.00

F.D.R. "Man of the Hour" Clock
Date: 1933 • Maker: United Clock Corp.
Franklin D. Roosevelt steering the nation
with the New Deal. Wind-up with double
animation. Boy's arm and ship's wheel move.
$200.00 – 300.00

Fireplace Clock
Date: 1950s • Maker: Mastercrafters
Fire in fireplace animated and
lights up. Case is early plastic.
$125.00 – 225.00

Fireplace Clock
Date: 1940s • Maker: United Clock Corp.
Sculptured man, woman, and child sit by lit fireplace.
Switch in back allows animation of fire and clock
to run independently. Electric with fancy metal case.
$175.00 – 275.00

Fireplace Clock
Date: 1950s • Maker: United Clock Corp.
Animation is moving flames in fireplace. Case is made
of wood and metal. Electrically lit fire and clock.
$125.00 – 250.00

Fireplace Clock
Date: 1940s • Maker: United Clock Corp.
Realistic looking fireplace showing burning logs.
Electric, no animation. Wooden case.
$75.00 – 150.00

Fireplace Clock
Date: 1940s • Maker: United Clock Corp.
Fancy silver colored metal case that surrounds
electric clock and fireplace, moving flames
make fireplace very realistic.
$175.00 – 275.00

Grandma "Home Sweet Home" Clock
Date: c. 1948 • Maker: Haddon
Grandmother rocking in front of glowing fire. Cottage
is made of dark brown pressed wood. Electric.
$175.00 – 250.00

Grandma Clock
Date: 1940s • Maker: Haddon
Scarce case made of brown syrocco wood. Grandma
rocks back and forth in front of glowing fire. Electric.
$200.00 – 300.00

Grandma Clock
Date: c. 1948 • Maker: Haddon
Scarce. Flowers adorn green cathedral type case.
Grandma rocks in front of glowing fire. Electric
movement lights up interior of room and fire.
$225.00 – 350.00

Hanson Cab Clock
Date: 1950s • Maker; United Clock Corp.
Carriage driver moves horse whip while
street lamp flickers. Electric animation.
$150.00 – 250.00

"Happy Time" Street Clock
Date: 1960s • Maker: Mastercrafters
Animated drunk with moving arm drinking
from his bottle, street lamp lights up.
$75.00 – 150.00

Huckleberry Finn Clock
Date: 1950s • Maker: United Clock Corp.
Double animation. Huck Finn moves fishing pole up and
down while fish swim in stream below. A turtle, fish, and
creel are embossed on gold colored metal.
$200.00 – 300.00

Hula Girl Clock
Date: 1930s • Maker: United Clock Corp.
Scarce. Double animation. Hula girl swings
hips while man plays bongo. Wood
case with fancy viewing window.
$250.00 – 450.00

Joe Louis Clock
Date: c. 1937 • Maker: United Clock Corp.
Scarce. Figural electric clock with no animation.
Great likeness of the ex-champ.
$500.00 – 800.00

Lighthouse Clock
Date: 1955 • Maker: United Clock Corp.
Man and woman are gazing at moving
sailboats, in revolving cylinder. Top of lighthouse
is lit as well as viewing window.
$250.00 – 375.00

Locomotive Clock
Date: 1950s • Maker: United Clock Corp.
No animation. Engineers cab lights up.
Sits on wooden base. Electric.
$75.00 – 150.00

Locomotive Clock
Date: 1950s • Maker: United Clock Corp.
Scarce. Realistic looking locomotive. Engineer's
arm is animated as he rings bell. Smokestack
and front of locomotive light up electrically.
$250.00 – 450.00

Majorette Clock
Date: 1950s • Maker: United Clock Corp.
Figural majorette twirls baton. Electric.
$150.00 – 250.00

McKinley Clock
Date: c. 1907 • Maker: Unknown
Scarce. Wind-up clock, no animation. Bust of William
McKinley. Sailor with cannon and soldier with rifle are
shown on clock case. Cast-iron clock commemorates his
assassination on September 14, 1901. His dying words
are inscribed on base, "It Is God's Way/His Will Be Done."
$300.00 – 475.00

Mermaid Clock
Date: c. 1948 • Maker: Sessions
Variation 1. Realistic fountain flows next to mermaid and
fish. Superb animation inside silver colored metal case.
$175.00 – 275.00

Mermaid Clock
Date: c. 1948 • Maker: Sessions
Variation 2. Gold colored metal case. Superb animation.
$175.00 – 275.00

Merry-Go-Round Clock
Date: 1950s • Maker: Mastercrafters
Animated using Sessions movement. Four
children ride carousel animals with ticket-taker
as merry-go-round revolves.
$250.00 – 450.00

Niagara Falls Clock
Date: 1950s • Maker: Mastercrafters
Scarce. Early plastic case with animated
waterfall, reminds one of Niagara Falls. Electric.
$220.00 – 350.00

Pluto Electric Clock
Date: 1950s • Maker: Allied Mfg. Co.
Variation 1. Disney's Pluto with double animation.
Eyes and tongue move. Dog bones act as clock
hands. Eyes and bones glow in the dark.
Came in white or yellow early plastic.
$250.00 – 450.00

Pluto Electric Clock
Date: 1950s • Maker: Allied Mfg. Co.
Variation 2. Disney's Pluto advertising
Vitality Dog Food. Dog bones and eyes
glow in the dark. Double animation.
$250.00 – 450.00

Pot Belly Stove Clock
Date: 1950s • Maker: United Clock Corp.
Moving fire shown through stove window.
Metal stove with electric movement.
$100.00 – 200.00

Ranch-O Clock
Date: 1950s • Maker: Haddon
Scenic diorama with bucking horse and rider.
Case is made of pressed wood similar to Davy
Crockett. Electric movement with lit scenery.
$175.00 – 275.00

Repeal Clock
Date: 1933 • Maker: United Clock Corp.
Scarce. Super sculptured metal case showing people
enjoying the repeal of Prohibition. Wind-up clock
is animated showing bartender mixing drink.
$275.00 – 400.00

Ship-Ahoy Clock
Date: 1940s • Maker: Haddon
Looking through the porthole at a schooner moving
in the waves. Attractive looking wooden case. Electric.
$250.00 – 375.00

Statue of Liberty Clock
Date: c. 1955 • Maker: United Clock Corp.
Scarce. People are shown gazing at various
moving boats near the Statue of Liberty. Attractive
metal case. Electric revolving cylinder.
$200.00 – 450.00

Steersmen of U.S.A. Clock
Date: 1933 • Maker: United Clock Corp.
Gold colored case showing Abraham Lincoln,
Franklin D. Roosevelt, and George Washington.
Metal case with wind-up movement. No animation.
$250.00 – 375.00

Sweethearts Clock
Date: 1934 • Maker: United Clock Corp.
Scarce. Also called Sally Rand Fan Dancer clock.
Animated fan. Figural of sweethearts kissing above
heart. Cream colored painted metal case. Wind-up.
$300.00 – 400.00

Swinging Bird Clock
Date: 1950s • Maker: Mastercrafters
Desirable green early plastic case with swinging
bird in cage. Sessions electrical movement.
$200.00 – 300.00

Swinging Playmates Clock
Date: 1950s • Maker: Mastercrafters
Boy and girl swing on separate swings.
Colorful background. Electrical movement.
$125.00 – 250.00

Teeter-Totter Clock
Date: 1950s • Maker: Haddon
Boy and girl move on teeter-totter, early plastic case
with realistic background. Diorama lit electrically.
$175.00 – 275.00

Waterfall Clock
Date: 1950s • Maker: Mastercrafter
Animated realistic waterfall. Early
brown plastic case. Electric.
$150.00 – 250.00

Waterfall Clock
Date: 1950s • Maker: Mastercrafter
Variant green colored case with realistic waterfall.
$150.00 – 250.00

Will Rogers Clock
Date: 1930s • Maker: United Clock Corp.
Three embossed statues of Will Rogers adorn
metal case. Shows Will Rogers as radio star and
movie actor. Larger bust has him wearing his typical
hat. Clock is hand wound with no animation.
$200.00 – 300.00

Windmill Clock
Date: 1950s • Maker: United Clock Corp.
Seldom seen animated windmill clock. Young
girl is seen crossing the stream. Electric.
$175.00 – 275.00

Boudoir or Desk Clocks

Bell Tower Clock
Date: 1900s • Maker: Swiss
Scarce. Hand-painted porcelain dial measuring 1¾"
diameter. Clock located in bell tower of church
with moving tiny bell in steeple. Clock attached
to black onyx or marble base with brass ball feet.
$450.00 – 750.00

Blacksmith Clock
Date: 1900s • Maker: France
Scarce. Animated metal blacksmith with moving mallet.
Metal dial surrounded by beaded bezel. Metal flowered
feet attach clock to gray onyx or marble base.
$350.00 – 550.00

Cherub Clock — Le Petit Forgeron
Date: 1900s • Maker: Swiss (Brevet & Depose)
Scarce. One animated cherub forging arrows.
Clock case is brass with black onyx or marble
base. Metal dial with 1¾" diameter face.
$375.00 – 600.00

Cherub Clock — Le Petit Forgeron
Date: 1900s • Maker: Swiss
Scarce. Hand-painted 1¾" dial with beaded bezel.
Animated cherub forging arrow. Clock rests on
green onyx or marble base with two rose
carved ball feet holding clock to base.
$375.00 – 600.00

Cherubs Clock
Date: 1900s • Maker: France
Scarce. Two hand-painted cherubs on 1¾"
porcelain dial, animation is one gold colored cherub
forging arrows. Clock rests on brass platform
and brass ball feet. Swiss movement.
$450.00 – 750.00

Magician Clock
Date: 1900s • Maker: France (Fab Suisse)
Rare. Magician is hand painted on ivory or sea
shell. Clock is 4" high and 2¾" wide. An egg and
ace of club card are held by magician. When button
above magician's head is pressed and held down,
the hour and minutes appear in the little windows.
The yogi or magician is behind glass. The square
brass Swiss movement clock is attached to an
ornate base. Two ruby-red like stones adorn
the silver and marble or onyx pedestal base.
$1,300.00 – 2,800.00

Mansion Clock
Date: 1900s • Maker: France
Scarce. Mansion scene hand painted on ivory or sea shell.
Time revolves in back of country scene on disc. Tall tree
acts as pointer on stationary face. Only four hours show at
a time as disc revolves. Unique clock is nickel plated on a
light green onyx base. Dial is 1¾" diameter.
$375.00 – 600.00

Silk Maker Clock
Date: 1930s • Maker: Swiss (Geneve)
Giesha girl is spinning silk. Animated
in 1¾" diameter dial. Clock is housed
in green Catalin case with easel back.
$150.00 – 225.00

Category 6
Comic Watches

Alice in Wonderland Wristwatch
Date: 1950 • Maker: U.S. Time
Disney character watch came with picture
of Alice wearing apron, packaged in plastic
tea cup. Colorful round box.
Watch only $60.00 – 125.00
Box only (scarce) $200.00 – 400.00

Alice in Wonderland Wristwatch
Date: 1953 • Maker: New Haven
Animated Disney Mad Hatter at 6:00 position.
$100.00 – 175.00

Alice in Wonderland Wristwatch
Date: 1958 • Maker: Timex
Scarce. Plastic statue with watch bearing word "Alice."
Also in series, with just words on face were Mickey
Mouse, Donald Duck, Cinderella, and Snow White.
Watch only $50.00 – 90.00
Statue only $50.00 – 95.00

Alice in Wonderland Wristwatch
Date: 1958 • Maker: Timex
Scarce. Ceramic statue with display stand.
Watch dial has "Alice" on it.
Watch only $50.00 – 90.00
Statue with stand only $125.00 – 225.00

Alice in Wonderland Wristwatch
Date: 1958 • Maker: Timex
Close-up of watch that bears Alice's name.
$50.00 – 90.00

Alice in Wonderland Wristwatch
Date: 1972 • Maker: Wotania (Swiss)
Animated Disney Mad Hatter at
8:00 position. Gold-toned case.
$60.00 – 125.00

Ballerina Wristwatch
Date: 1963 • Maker: Bradley
Pink vinyl wristband. Gold-toned case
on watch. Packaged in plastic box.
Watch only $70.00 – 100.00
Box only $75.00 – 125.00

Ballerina Wristwatch
Date: 1968 • Maker: Bradley
Variation having gold-toned aluminum case.
$75.00 – 125.00

Ballerina Reflector Strips
Date: 1960 Maker: Ingraham (Optical Animation)
Scarce. Unused hologram reflector strips
that could be put on dial. Seven images
gave appearance of ballerina moving.
Strip only $75.00 – 150.00

Bambi "Birthday Series" Box
Date: 1948 • Maker: Ingersoll
Birthday Series box, ten Disney characters on
box lid. These characters are Mickey Mouse,
Donald Duck, Bambi, Pinocchio, Jiminy Cricket,
Bongo, Joe Carioca, Daisy Duck, Dopey, and Pluto.
Same box design used all on ten characters.
Box only $100.00 – 175.00

Bambi Wristwatch
Date: 1949 • Maker: Ingersoll (U.S. Time)
Outer circle and ears are luminous. Ears act as minute
and hour hands. Seven out of ten Disney characters
were also made luminous in 1949. Luminous box
models contained a place for ballpoint pen.
Watch only $175.00 – 300.00
Luminous box only $180.00 – 325.00

Bambi Wristwatch
Date: 1949 • Maker: Ingersoll (U.S. Time)
Close-up of luminous Bambi produced in 1949.
Luminous ears act as hour and minute hands.
$175.00 – 300.00

Blondie Wristwatch
Date: 1949 • Maker: King Features Syndicate
Scarce. Blondie, Dagwood, Daisy, and her
pup show on dial. Has metal link band.
$400.00 – 600.00

Blondie Wristwatch
Date: 1949 • Maker: King Features Syndicate
Rare. Cookie, Alexander, Daisy,
and her pup show on dial.
$500.00 – 800.00

Bongo Wristwatch
Date: 1948 • Maker: Ingersoll (U.S. Time)
Part of original birthday series, celebrates twentieth
birthday of Mickey Mouse. Bongo inside circle,
arms and hands act as hour and minute hands.
Watch only $175.00 – 300.00
Box only $150.00 – 300.00

Bongo Wristwatch
Date: 1948 • Maker: Ingersoll (U.S. Time)
Close-up of Disney Bongo the Bear.
$175.00 – 300.00

Bongo Wristwatch
Date: 1949 • Maker: Ingersoll (U.S. Time)
A larger Bongo outside the inner circle.
Non-luminous. Starred in "Fun and Fancy Free."
$175.00 – 300.00

Bugs Bunny Wristwatch
Date: 1951 • Maker: Rexall Drugs
Variation 1. Two carrots are the hour and minute hands.
$185.00 – 300.00

Bugs Bunny Wristwatch
Date: 1951 • Maker: Rexall Drugs
Variation 2. Warner Bros. Bugs Bunny with orange
hands instead of carrot hands.
$165.00 – 250.00

Bugs Bunny Wristwatch
Date: 1951 • Maker: Rexall Drugs
Variation 3. Bugs Bunny holds carrot stalk with two
green luminous hands.
$165.00 – 250.00

Buster Brown Wristwatch
Date: 1975 • Maker: Buster Brown Shoe Co.
Watch with original papers. Inside
of lid has Buster Brown and Tige.
Watch only $50.00 – 95.00
Box only $35.00 – 75.00

Buster Brown Wristwatch
Date: 1975 • Maker: Buster Brown Shoe co.
Colorful watch with animated hands.
$50.00 – 95.00

Cinderella Wristwatch
Date: 1950s • Maker: Timex
Scarce. Box resembles book. Horses,
footmen, and Cinderella are shown on
outside of unique box. Sold at Disneyland.
Box only $350.00 – 500.00

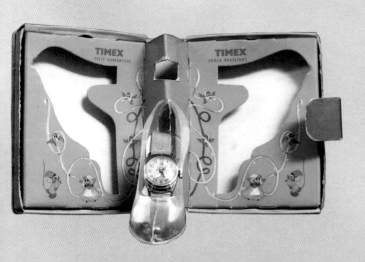

Cinderella Wristwatch
Date: 1950s • Maker: Timex
Scarce. Book-type box open to show
Cinderella wristwatch in plastic slipper.
Small cardboard tabs act as book latch.
Watch and slipper only $100.00 – 200.00
Box only $350.00 – 500.00

Cinderella Wristwatch
Date: 1950 • Maker: U.S. Time
Disney's Cinderella in round slipper
box. Watch in plastic slipper.
Watch and slipper only $100.00 – 200.00
Box only $350.00 – 450.00

Cinderella Wristwatch
Date: 1950 • Maker: U.S. Time
Cinderella in bluish square box.
Watch and slipper only $100.00 – 200.00
Box only $375.00 – 475.00

Cinderella Wristwatch
Date: 1955 • Maker: Timex
Scarce. Black and pink box lid for Cinderella watch.
Box with animation cell $275.00 – 400.00

Cinderella Wristwatch
Date: 1955 • Maker: Timex
Scarce. Cinderella watch inside box with
movie scene. Resembles an animation cell.
Watch only $75.00 – 125.00
Box with animation cell $275.00 – 400.00

Cinderella Wristwatch
Date: 1958 • Maker: Timex
Plastic statue of Cinderella on display
stand. Watch dial has words.
Watch only $75.00 – 125.00
Display stand and statue only $100.00 – 175.00

Cinderella Wristwatch
Date: 1958 • Maker: Timex
Close-up of "Cinderella" name.
$45.00 – 75.00

Cinderella Wristwatch
Date: 1958 • Maker: Timex
Cinderella porcelain statue with watch
Dial has Cinderella running from castle.
Watch only $75.00 – 100.00
Statue only $35.00 – 50.00

Cinderella Wristwatch
Date: 1971 • Maker: Bradley
Gold-toned bezel with expansion band.
Cinderella in pink gown.
$50.00 – 75.00

Cinderella Wristwatch
Date: 1972 • Maker: Bradley
Light blue long gloves act as watch hands.
Darker blue background.
$50.00 – 85.00

Cinderella Wristwatch
Date: 1972 • Maker: Webster (New York)
Animated shoe at 7:00 position.
$45.00 – 75.00

Daffy Duck Wristwatch
Date: 1971 • Maker: Sheraton
Part of a series with Cool Cat, Elmer Fudd,
Wile E. Coyote, Porky Pig, and Roadrunner.
$175.00 – 275.00

Daisy Duck Wristwatch
Date: 1947 • Maker: Ingersoll
Colorful post war Disney watch with rectangular case.
Daisy with animated hands.
$200.00 – 300.00

Daisy Duck Wristwatch
Date: 1948 • Maker: Ingersoll
One of ten birthday watches commemorating Mickey
Mouse's twentieth birthday. Watch has round case.
Watch only $200.00 – 300.00
Box only $150.00 – 300.00

Daisy Duck Wristwatch
Date: 1948 • Maker: Ingersoll
Close-up of Disney's Daisy the Duck.
Daisy shown inside circle on dial.
$200.00 – 300.00

Dick Tracy Wristwatch
Date: 1935 • Maker: New Haven
Variation 1. Watch hands are red, hat is blue.
Watch is smaller than variation 2. Full figure.
$250.00 – 375.00

Dick Tracy Wristwatch
Date: 1935 • Maker: New Haven
Variation 2. Black watch hands. Hat is brown.
Rectangular case is slightly larger, full figure.
$250.00 – 375.00

Dick Tracy Wristwatch
Date: 1948 • Maker: New Haven
Round case has horn-like bezel. Unique style bezel
is similar to Superman and Little Orphan Annie.
$225.00 – 325.00

Dick Tracy Wristwatch
Date: 1948 • Maker: New Haven
Partial shot of Tracy holding automatic
gun. "Dick Tracy" words moved to above
his knees. Colorful box and insert.
Watch only $200.00 – 300.00
Box only $300.00 – 500.00

Dick Tracy Wristwatch
Date: 1951 • Maker: New Haven
Animated western gun. Early version (1948) used auto-
matic style gun. This version used Gene Autry six-shoot-
er, as pictured. Came in slimmer white box.
Watch only $200.00 – 400.00
Box only $400.00 – 600.00

Donald Duck Wristwatch
Date: 1947 • Maker: Ingersoll
Rectangular silver-toned case with ornate bezel. Disney's
Donald Duck hands are hour and minute hands.
$275.00 – 400.00

Donald Duck Wristwatch
Date: 1947 • Maker: Ingersoll
Deluxe gold-toned bezel. $1.00 more at time.
$300.00 – 450.00

Donald Duck Wristwatch
Date: 1947 • Maker: Ingersoll/U.S. Time
Scarce. Donald Duck wristwatch, ballpoint pen, and
ring displayed in attractive birthday cake box.
Commemorated Mickey Mouse's twentieth birthday.
Complete package $700.00 – 1,100.00

Donald Duck Wristwatch
Date: 1947 • Maker: Ingersoll/U.S. Time
Scarce. Top of birthday cake
box with a place for candles.
Complete package $700.00 – 1,100.00

Donald Duck Wristwatch
Date: 1949 • Maker: Ingersoll/U.S. Time
Donald Duck Wristwatch shown in birthday series box,
celebrating Mickey Mouse's twentieth birthday. Series
included ten Disney characters as shown on box lid.
Watch only $250.00 – 375.00
Box only $150.00 – 300.00

Donald Duck Wristwatch
Date: 1949 • Maker: Ingersoll/U.S. Time
Close-up of Disney's Donald Duck in box. Donald is
outside of inner circle on dial, making it a year later than
1948 model. Original blue vinylite band with $6.95 foil.
$250.00 – 375.00

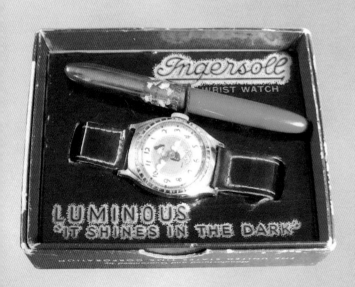

Donald Duck Wristwatch
Date: 1949 • Maker: Ingersoll/U.S. Time
Seven out of ten Disney characters in birthday
series were made luminous. A small Donald
Duck ballpoint pen came in this box.
Watch only $250.00 – 375.00
Luminous box only $200.00 – 350.00

Donald Duck Wristwatch
Date: 1949 • Maker: Ingersoll/U.S. Time
Close-up of luminous Disney Donald Duck.
Fluted bezel. Luminous or glow-in-the-dark hands
were common after World War II.
Watch only $250.00 – 375.00
Luminous box only $200.00 – 350.00

Donald Duck Wristwatch
Date: 1955 • Maker: U.S. Time
Scarce. Pop-up box of Disney's Donald
Duck. Decorative box. Animated hands.
Watch only $150.00 – 225.00
Box only $300.00 – 450.00

Donald Duck Wristwatch
Date: 1959 • Maker: U.S. Time
"Donald Duck" words only, watch on
Donald Duck ceramic statue.
Watch only $50.00 – 75.00
Statue only $65.00 – 95.00

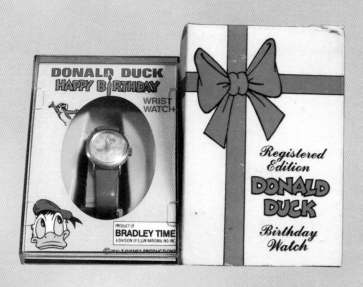

Donald Duck Wristwatch
Date: 1984 • Maker: Bradley Time
Commemorated Donald Duck's fiftieth birthday.
$100.00 – 150.00

Dopey Wristwatch
Date: 1948 • Maker: Ingersoll/U.S. Time
One of ten watches commemorating
Mickey Mouse's twentieth birthday.
Watch only $175.00 – 300.00
Box only $150.00 – 300.00

Dopey Wristwatch
Date: 1948 • Maker: Ingersoll/U.S. Time
Close-up of Disney's Dopey from Snow
White. Dopey with animated hands.
$175.00 – 300.00

Fiddler Pig (Little Pig) Wristwatch
Date: 1947 • Maker: Ingersoll
Little Pig or Fiddler Pig. One of four early
post-war watches including Fiddler Pig, Danny
the Lamb, Louie the Duck, and Snow White.
$250.00 – 375.00

Goofy (Backwards) Wristwatch
Date: 1972 • Maker: Helbros
Scarce. Seventeen jeweled watch. Numbers and hands
run backwards. Discontinued after limited production.
Watch instruction confused children.
$400.00 – 800.00

Goofy (Backwards) Wristwatch
Date: 1990s • Maker: Lorus (Japan)
Walt Disney Productions, made
in Japan. Quartz movement.
$75.00 – 125.00

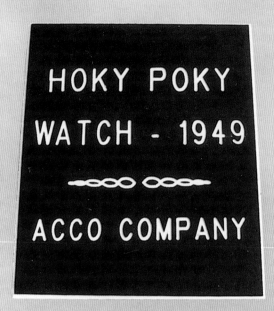

Hoky Poky Watch Sign

Hoky Poky Wristwatch
Date: 1949 • Maker: Acco Co.
Rare. Box has cellophane window showing watch with
visible motion. Watch has blue early vinyl wristband.
Watch only $500.00 – 700.00
Box only $250.00 – 350.00

Hoky Poky Wristwatch
Date: 1949 • Maker: Acco Co.
Rare. Close-up of magician with moving arm
creating illusion of egg changing to chick and
cards changing place, looks like double
movement. Hands and numbers glow in the dark.
$500.00 – 700.00

Howdy Doody Wristwatch
Date: 1954 • Maker: Patent Watch Co.
Rare. Eyes move as watch ticks. Close-up
of Howdy Doody face on watch shows
through cellophane window.
Watch only $275.00 – 400.00
Box only $275.00 – 400.00

Howdy Doody Wristwatch
Date: 1954 • Maker: Ingraham
Scarce. Close-up of Howdy Doody, Clarabelle,
Princess Summerfall Winterspring, and Dilly Dally.
$275.00 – 400.00

Jiminy Cricket Wristwatch
Date: 1948 • Maker: Ingersoll/U.S. Time
One of ten Disney watches commemorating
Mickey Mouse's twentieth birthday.
Watch only $175.00 – 300.00
Box only $150.00 – 300.00

Jiminy Cricket Wristwatch
Date: 1949 • Maker: Ingersoll/U.S. Time
Close-up of Jiminy's feet outside of
inner circle making it one year later.
$250.00 – 375.00

Joe Carioca Wristwatch
Date: 1948 • Maker: Ingersoll/U.S. Time
Scarce. Watch with gold-toned bezel is deluxe version of
birthday series. Watch came with special horizontal box.
Watch only $350.00 – 500.00
Box only $200.00 – 300.00

Joe Carioca Wristwatch
Date: 1948 • Maker: Ingersoll/U.S. Time
Close-up of Joe Carioca deluxe birthday watch.
$350.00 – 500.00

Joe Carioca Wristwatch
Date: 1953 • Maker: Unknown
Scarce. Colorful dial. Animated hands.
$175.00 – 375.00

Joe Palooka Wristwatch
Date: 1947 • Maker: New Haven
Popular comic strip character.
$200.00 – 400.00

Junior Nurse Wristwatch
Date: 1956 • Maker: Ingraham
Comic career watch.
$75.00 – 125.00

Li'l Abner Wristwatch
Date: 1951 • Maker: New Haven
Variation 1. Large facial shot of
Li'l Abner with animated flag. Colorful box.
Watch only $275.00 – 375.00
Box only $400.00 – 600.00

Li'l Abner Wristwatch
Date: 1951 • Maker: New Haven
Close-up of Li'l Abner with animated
flag. Hands and numbers glow-in-the-dark.
$275.00 – 375.00

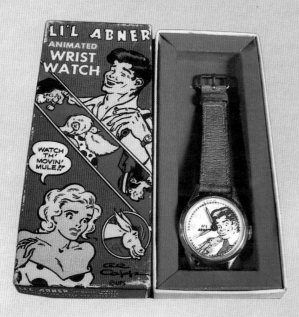

Li'l Abner Wristwatch
Date: 1951 • Maker: New Haven
Variation 2. Scarce. Watch with
animated mule instead of flag. Variant box showing
Daisy Mae exclaiming "Watch th' movin' mule!"
Watch only $300.00 – 400.00
Box only $450.00 – 650.00

Li'l Abner Wristwatch
Date: 1951 • Maker: New Haven
Scarce. Close-up of moving mule.
$300.00 – 400.00

Li'l Abner Wristwatch
Date: 1951 • Maker: New Haven
Variation 3. Smaller portrait
of Li'l Abner saluting with animated flag.
$275.00 – 375.00

Li'l Abner Wristwatch
Date: 1955 • Maker: U.S.F.
Rare. Sketch of Li'l Abner with words "Li'l Abner"
on dial. Smaller than other Li'l Abner watches.
$200.00 – 300.00

Lucy Wristwatch
Date: 1974 • Maker: Timex
United Features Syndicate Peanuts
cartoon. Not to be confused with earlier Bradley model.
$75.00 – 125.00

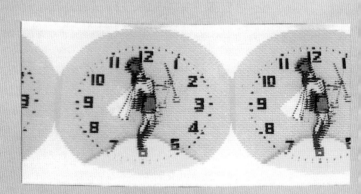

Majorette Reflector Strip
Date: 1960 • Maker: Ingraham
Scarce. Each strip has seven identical characters. Reflector face gives appearance of arm and baton moving, acting as early hologram. Strips were made for Roy Rogers, Dale Evans, ballerina, and majorette.
Strip only $75.00 – 150.00

Merlin the Magic Mouse Wristwatch
Date: 1971 • Maker: Sheffield
Merlin the Magic Mouse, Daffy Duck, Popeye,
Porky Pig, and Felix the Cat are in the same series.
$125.00 – 225.00

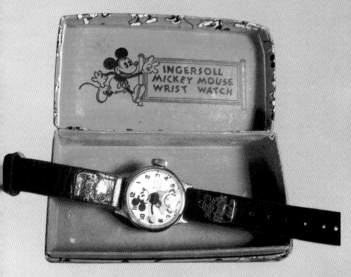

Mickey Mouse Wristwatch
Date: 1933 • Maker: Ingersoll
Characters illustrated on the outside of the
"Critter" box include Mickey Mouse, Minnie Mouse,
Horace Horsecollar, Pluto, and Clarabelle the Cow.
Watch only $300.00 – 700.00
Box only $150.00 – 300.00

Mickey Mouse Wristwatch
Date: 1933 • Maker: Ingersoll
Leather watch band with two Mickey
appliqués. Second hand at 6:00 position
has three Mickeys chasing each other.
$300.00 – 700.00

Mickey Mouse Wristwatch
Date: 1935 • Maker: Ingersoll
Blue box replaces Critter box with price
reduction from $3.75 to $2.95.
Watch only $400.00 – 800.00
Box only $200.00 – 325.00

Mickey Mouse Wristwatch
Date: 1935 • Maker: Ingersoll
"Made in U.S.A." was added near the 8:00 position. This
helped deter counterfeiting and increase foreign sales.
$400.00 – 800.00

Mickey Mouse Wristwatch
Date: 1937 – 1938 • Maker: Ingersoll
Rare. One Mickey running at 6:00 position for
second hand. Boys watch with leather band.
Box sometimes called the "Fred Astaire" version,
since Mickey pictured with top hat and coat.
Watch only $400.00 – 800.00.
Box only $1,600.00 – 2,500.00

Mickey Mouse Wristwatch
Date: 1937 – 1938 • Maker: Ingersoll
Rare. Inside of Fred Astaire box shows
Mickey after a night on the town.

Mickey Mouse Wristwatch
Date: 1937 – 1938 • Maker: Ingersoll
Rare. Hinged box shows girl's watch with link band.
Watch only $600.00 – 800.00
Hinged box only $1,700.00 – 2,600.00

Mickey Mouse Wristwatch
Date: 1937 – 1938 • Maker: Ingersoll
One running Mickey instead
of three act as second hand.
$600.00 – 800.00

Mickey Mouse Paperwork
Date: 1937 – 1938 • Maker: Ingersoll
Ingersoll guarantee slip. Final payment slip for
lay-away from October 17, 1938, and $2.00 off slip
from store in Setee, Texas, all for girl's hinged box.
$25.00 – 45.00

Mickey Mouse Wristwatch
Date: 1939 • Maker: Ingersoll
Watch price reduced to $3.25 from $3.95.
Different leather and link bands were offered
with this watch. A regular plain second hand
used instead of Mickeys. Fluted bezel.
Watch only $200.00 – 300.00
Box only $150.00 – 250.00

Mickey Mouse Wristwatch
Date: 1939 • Maker: Ingersoll
Deluxe gold-plated fluted bezel. Second hand
used numerals instead of moving Mickeys.
Models came in rectangular case instead of round.
Gold-plated version sold for $1.00 more.
$250.00 – 350.00

Mickey Mouse Wristwatch
Date: 1939 • Maker: Ingersoll
Unique black silk cord on this girl's
version. Bezel fluted with chrome plating.
$200.00 – 300.00

Mickey Mouse Wristwatch
Date: 1939 • Maker: Ingersoll
Watch is rather plain. No fluting on bezel. Leather band.
$175.00 – 275.00

Kelton Wristwatch
Date: 1946 • Maker: Kelton
Post-war watch before Mickey was added to the dial.
$75.00 – 125.00

Mickey Mouse Wristwatch
Date: 1946 • Maker: Kelton
Scarce. Mickey Mouse's face and arms on rotating
plastic dial. First post-war Mickey Mouse watch.
$250.00 – 450.00

Mickey Mouse Wristwatch
Date: 1947 • Maker: Ingersoll
Rectangular chromium bezel. Mickey
standing. Original foil $6.95 tag on
wristband. Colorful yellow box and insert.
Watch only $150.00 – 250.00
Box only $150.00 – 250.00

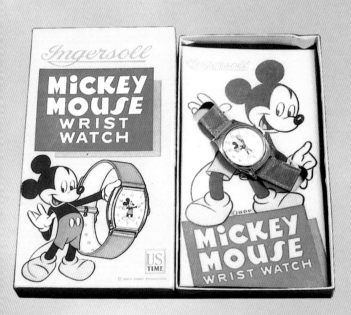

Mickey Mouse Wristwatch
Date: 1947 • Make: Ingersoll
Round watch in colorful box instead of rectangular.
Watch only $150.00 – 250.00
Box only $150.00 – 250.00

Mickey Mouse Wristwatch
Date: 1947 • Maker: Ingersoll
Close-up of large round Mickey Mouse watch.
$150.00 – 250.00

Mickey Mouse Wristwatch
Date: 1947 • Maker: Ingersoll/U.S. Time
Gold-toned deluxe Mickey Mouse. Sold for
$1.00 more. Scarce maroon box.
Watch only $200.00 – 300.00
Box only $200.00 – 300.00

Mickey Mouse Wristwatch
Date: 1940s • Maker: Ingersoll
Scarce. Extra large size with red numerals.
Fancy bezel with link band. Possibly English.
$200.00 – 400.00

Mickey Mouse Birthday Cake Style
Date: 1947 • Maker: U.S. Time
Rare. Rectangular watch with added
Donald Duck ballpoint pen and Pluto ring
nestled in blue velvet type material.
Complete package $700.00 – 1,100.00

Mickey Mouse Birthday Cake Style
Date: 1947 • Maker: U.S. Time
Rare. White early plastic hinged birthday cake
box. Celebrates Mickey's twentieth birthday. On
top of box lid, in pink, is written "Happy Birthday."
Six candles can be inserted into the lid.
Complete package $700.00 – 1,100.00

Mickey Mouse Wristwatch
Date: 1949 • Maker: Ingersoll/U.S. Time
Commemorates Mickey Mouse's twentieth
birthday. Other watches in series include
Donald Duck, Daisy Duck, Jiminy Cricket, Bongo,
Pluto, Bambi, Joe Carioca, Pinocchio, and
Dopey. Ten characters pictured on box lid.
Watch only $375.00 – 475.00
Box only $125.00 – 225.00

Mickey Mouse Wristwatch
Date: 1949 • Maker: Ingersoll/U.S. Time
Close-up of larger image of Mickey with feet outside of
inner circle. Fluting on case at 6:00 and 12:00 position.
$375.00 – 475.00

Mickey Mouse Wristwatch
Date: 1952 • Maker: U.S. Time
Scarce. Oval box with die cut of Mickey
holding watch. Box lid shows Mickey, Minnie,
Donald Duck and Nephews, and Pluto.
Watch only $125.00 – 225.00
Box with die cut only $275.00 – 400.00

Mickey Mouse Wristwatch
Date: 1952 • Maker: U.S. Time
Close-up of Mickey with animated
hands. Round chromium case.
$125.00 – 225.00

Mickey Mouse Wristwatch
Date: 1958 • Maker: U.S. Time
Plastic Mickey statue on heavy cardboard.
Mickey with red vinylite band.
Watch only $125.00 – 225.00
Statue and stand only $175.00 – 275.00

Mickey Mouse Wristwatch
Date: 1958 • Maker: U.S. Time
Close-up of Mickey with black numerals.
Last watches to have "Ingersoll" printed on face.
$125.00 – 225.00

Mickey Mouse Wristwatch
Date: 1958 • Maker: U.S. Time
Close-up of Mickey watch with his name only.
This is one of a series of five that had names only,
Donald Duck, Alice, Snow White, and Cinderella.
Came on porcelain statue of Mickey.
150.00 – 250.00

Mickey Mouse Wristwatch
Date: 1950s • Maker: U.S. Time
Red plastic round bezel. Ingersoll words
removed from face. Numerals in red.
$75.00 – 125.00

Mickey Mouse Wristwatch
Date: 1950s • Maker: U.S. Time
Rectangular watch. Red numerals. Ingersoll removed.
$75.00 – 125.00

Mickey Mouse Wristwatch
Date: 1966 • Maker: Unknown
Scarce. Unusual version of Mickey with tongue
sticking out. Yellow band with cut-out hearts.
$175.00 – 275.00

Mickey Mouse Display
Date: 1960s • Maker: Unknown
Handsome display for Disney watches. Mickey
Mouse's head moves back and forth. Uses batteries.
$175.00 – 250.00

Mickey Mouse Wristwatch
Date: 1968 • Maker: Timex
Animated hands. Watch in black Ingersoll hinged box.
Watch only $90.00 – 135.00
Box only $40.00 – 60.00

Mickey Mouse Wristwatch
Date: 1970s • Maker: Bradley
Small watch with regular hands
instead of Mickey hands.
$75.00 – 125.00

Mickey Mouse Wristwatch
Date: 1973 • Maker: Bradley
Time-teacher with blue face and red vinyl band. Small
picture of Mickey between 11:00 and 12:00 position.
$145.00 – 175.00

Mickey Mouse Wristwatch
Date: 1974 • Maker: Webster
Animated flower at 7:00 position.
$75.00 – 125.00

Mickey Mouse Wristwatch
Date: 1978 • Maker: Bradley
Issued during Mickey Mouse Club revival on TV.
$95.00 – 140.00

Mickey Mouse Wristwatch
Date: 1978 • Maker: Bradley
Moving head. Other moving heads
in series are Minnie and Pluto.
$125.00 – 175.00

Mickey Mouse Wristwatch
Date: 1960s • Maker: Louis Marx
Toy watch with animated feet.
$45.00 – 75.00

Minnie Mouse Wristwatch
Date: 1958 • Maker: U.S. Time
Plastic statue with Minnie Mouse watch. First
appearance of Minnie on a watch. Animated hands.
Watch only $75.00 – 125.00
Statue and stand only $150.00 – 200.00
Box cover only $50.00 – 75.00

Minnie Mouse Wristwatch
Date: 1958 • Maker: U.S. Time
Scarce. Plastic Minnie in plastic frame.
Watch attached to cardboard easel.
Original foil tag of $7.95 on watch band.
Watch only $75.00 – 125.00
Frame and stand only $200.00 – 250.00
Box cover only $50.00 – 75.00

Minnie Mouse Statue
Date: 1958 • Maker: U.S. Time
Porcelain watch statue.
$45.00 – 65.00

Minnie Mouse Wristwatch
Date: 1968 • Maker: Timex
Large size watch with modern band.
$90.00 – 135.00

New Haven Character Watch Display
Date: 1951 • Maker: New Haven
Rare. N.O.S. (new old stock) display. Features three
animated Li'L Abner and three animated Dick Tracy.
Each watch cost $6.95. Some displays feature
animated Gene Autry and animated Annie Oakley.
$2,200.00 – 3,600.00

Orphan Annie (Little) Box
Date: 1935 • Maker: New Haven
Pictured on the rectangular box is Orphan
Annie, Sandy, and Daddy Warbucks.
$175.00 – 250.00

Orphan Annie (Little) Wristwatch
Date: 1935 • Maker: New Haven
Variation 1. Large uncommon version.
Chromium case with leather band.
$200.00 – 300.00

Orphan Annie (Little) Wristwatch
Date: 1935 • Maker: New Haven
Variation 2. Smaller version of Little Orphan
Annie watch. Inside of lid has advertising blurb.
Watch only $200.00 – 300.00
Box only $175.00 – 250.00

Orphan Annie (Little) Wristwatch
Date: 1948 • Maker: New Haven
Little Orphan Annie and Sandy appear on box lid and
stand-up insert. Style 1 is rectangular with leather band.
Watch only $125.00 – 175.00
Box and insert only $200.00 – 325.00

Orphan Annie (Little) Wristwatch
Date: 1948 • Maker: New Haven
Close-up of rectangular Little Orphan Annie watch.
$125.00 – 175.00

Orphan Annie (Little) Wristwatch
Date: 1948 • Maker: New Haven
Style 2, with Little Orphan Annie and
Sandy pictured with round case watch.
Watch only $150.00 – 200.00
Box only $200.00 – 325.00

Orphan Annie (Little) Wristwatch
Date: 1948 • Maker: New Haven
Round case with horn-like bezel.
Similar to Superman and Dick Tracy.
$150.00 – 200.00

Paul Bunyan Wristwatch
Date: 1948 • Maker: Muros Watch Factory
Scarce. Animated body. Companion piece to Annie
Oakley. Radium hands and numbers on dial.
$375.00 – 575.00

Peter Pan Toy Watch
Date: 1953 • Maker: Germany
Tin toy watch with vinyl strap. Attached to colorful card.
$35.00 – 55.00

Peter Pan Wristwatch
Date: 1974 • Maker: Webster
Animated Tinkerbell at 7:00 position.
$75.00 – 125.00

Piggy Wristwatch
Date: 1972 • Maker: Unknown
Animated head.
$75.00 – 125.00

Pinocchio Wristwatch
Date: 1948 • Maker: Ingersoll/U.S. Time
One of ten characters made to celebrate Mickey
Mouse's twentieth birthday. Including Jiminy Cricket,
Donald Duck, Daisy Duck, Dopey, Mickey Mouse,
Pluto, Joe Carioca, Bambi, and Bongo the Bear.
Watch only $175.00 – 200.00
Box only $150.00 – 300.00

Pinocchio Wristwatch
Date: 1948 • Maker: Ingersoll/U.S. Time
Pinocchio inside inner circle with animated hands.
Original foil price tag attached to red vinylite band.
$175.00 – 200.00

Pinocchio Wristwatch
Date: 1958 • Maker: U.S. Time
Scarce. Plastic statue with watch
attached to cardboard easel.
Watch only $175.00 – 275.00
Statue and stand only $225.00 – 325.00

Pinocchio Wristwatch
Date: 1958 • Maker: U.S. Time
Scarce. Close-up of Pinocchio
with strings and animated hands.
$175.00 – 275.00

Pinocchio Wristwatch
Date: 1974 • Maker: Webster
Animated Jiminy Cricket at 7:00 position.
$75.00 – 125.00

Pluto Wristwatch
Date: 1948 • Maker: Ingersoll/U.S. Time
One of ten characters celebrating Mickey Mouse's twenti-
eth birthday. Pluto inside circle with animated ears.
Watch only $175.00 – 200.00
Box only $150.00 – 300.00

Pluto Wristwatch
Date: 1948 • Maker: Ingersoll/U.S. Time
Close-up of Pluto inside inner circle.
Animated ears. Blue vinylite band.
$175.00 – 200.00

Pluto Wristwatch
Date: 1949 • Maker: Ingersoll/U.S. Time
Luminous dial and numbers. Also
glow-in-the-dark ears. Fancy bezel on case.
$175.00 – 300.00

Popeye Wristwatch
Date: 1935 • Maker: New Haven
Scarce. Large size rectangular case with
leather strap. Thimble Theater players are shown
on dial. Popeye, Olive Oyl, Wimpy, etc. Popeye's
hands and arms are animated. Wimpy as
second hand, chasing the elusive hamburger.
$550.00 – 800.00

Popeye Wristwatch
Date: 1948 • Maker: Unknown
Scarce. Large round case. Popeye, Olive
Oyl, Swee' Pea, and Wimpy shown on dial.
Possible unauthorized version.
$250.00 – 550.00

Popeye Wristwatch
Date: 1971 • Maker: Sheffield
Scarce. Animated hands. Popeye in running position.
Back of watch shows inner workings. Comes with
magnifier and booklet explaining how the watch works.
Colorful box with cellophane window showing watch.
Box lid show Popeye, Olive Oyl, Swee' Pea, Wimpy, and
Bluto. Sheffield series includes Merlin the Magic Mouse,
Daffy Duck, Porky Pig, and Felix the Cat.
Watch only $150.00 – 250.00
Box only $150.00 – 250.00

Porky Pig Wristwatch
Date: 1949 • Maker: Ingraham
Larger rectangular version. Chromium
case with animated hands.
$275.00 – 325.00

Porky Pig Wristwatch
Date: 1949 • Maker: Ingraham
Scarce. Colorful box with stand-up
insert showing Porky Pig holding small
version of watch with red leather band.
Watch only $275.00 – 325.00
Box with insert only $500.00 – 700.00

Porky Pig Wristwatch
Date: 1949 • Maker: Ingraham
Close-up of small version. "Porky Pig" name in
red rather than blue, as in rectangular version.
$275.00 – 325.00

Punkin Head Wristwatch
Date: 1947 • Maker: Ingraham
Prototype. Round version.
$125.00 – 200.00

Robin Hood Wristwatch
Date: 1956 • Maker: Bradley
Rectangular chromium case. Robin Hood facing
right holding bow and arrow. Fancy leather band.
$225.00 – 275.00

Robin Hood Wristwatch
Date: 1956 • Maker: Bradley
Rectangular gold-plated case. Deluxe version.
$250.00 – 300.00

Robin Hood Wristwatch
Date: 1958 • Maker: Viking
Scarce. Larger round style. Numerals and
hands glow in the dark. Bow is not extended.
$275.00 – 400.00

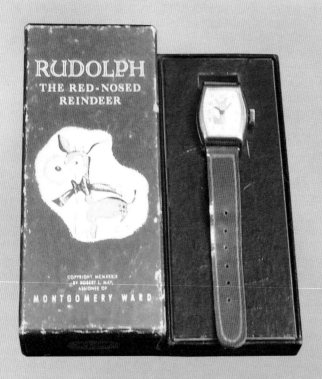

Rudolph (Red-Nosed Reindeer) Watch
Date: 1946 • Maker: Ingraham
Made for Montgomery Ward distribution.
Copyright 1939 by Robert L. May. Rudolph
pictured on watch and box lid.
Watch only $250.00 – 325.00
Box only $175.00 – 250.00

Rudolph (Red-Nosed Reindeer) Watch
Date: 1946 • Maker: Ingraham
Close-up of Rudolph on early version. facing toward
3:00 position. Lighted nose is not red. Red vinylite band.
$250.00 – 325.00

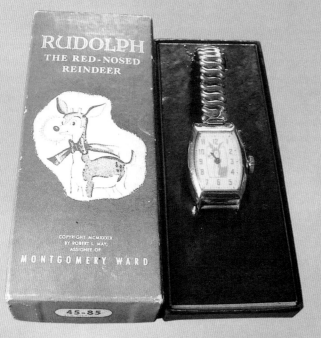

Rudolph (Red-Nosed Reindeer) Watch
Date: 1947 • Maker: Ingersoll
Same Wristwatch box used with different
stock number. Watch has expansion band.
Watch only $275.00 – 350.00
Box only $175.00 – 250.00

Rudolph (Red-Nosed Reindeer) Watch
Date: 1947 • Maker: Ingersoll
Close-up of Rudolph with red nose
facing towards 9:00 position.
$275.00 – 350.00

Smitty Wristwatch
Date: 1939 • Maker: Ingersoll
Scarce. Large rectangular chromium case. Smitty
wearing cap and sweater with knickers. Scarce
box showing Smitty with Herby on lid.
Watch only $250.00 – 350.00
Box only $225.00 – 300.00

Snoopy Wristwatch
Date: 1974 • Maker: Timex
Variation 1. Animated hands with yellow
sweep second hand. Red background.
$50.00 – 90.00

Snoopy Wristwatch
Date: 1974 • Maker: Timex
Variation 2. Animated hands with red
sweep second hand. Blue background.
$50.00 – 90.00

Snoopy Wristwatch
Date: 1976 • Maker: Timex
Snoopy with tennis racket. Second hand is animated
white tennis ball. Blue denim background with denim
strap. Acrylic box shaped like doghouse.
Watch only $60.00 – 110.00
Box only $40.00 – 75.00

Snoopy Wristwatch
Date: 1977 • Maker: Timex
Snoopy with tennis racket. Second hand is
animated green tennis ball. Yellow plastic strap.
$60.00 – 90.00

Snow White Wristwatch
Date: 1947 • Maker: Ingersoll
Scarce. Rectangular series in 1947 included
Snow White, Danny the Lamb, Little Pig
(Fiddler Pig), and Louie the Duck.
$225.00 – 300.00

Snow White Wristwatch
Date: 1948 • Maker: Ingersoll/U.S. Time
Scarce. Watch produced again with
round case. Bezel has fluted edge.
$175.00 – 250.00

Snow White Wristwatch
Date: 1950 • Maker: Ingersoll/U.S. Time
Round chromium case with red fabric strap.
Oval box with seven dwarfs pictured on lid.
Reflective insert resembles Magic Mirror. Variation 1,
plastic insert has Snow White written on it.
Watch only $75.00 – 125.00.
Scarce box and insert only $200.00 – 400.00

Snow White Wristwatch
Date: 1950 • Maker: Ingersoll/U.S. Time
Round chromium case with red fabric strap.
Oval box has "Snow White" written on lid.
Reflective insert resembles Magic Mirror.
Variation 2, plastic insert has "Ingersoll" written on it.
Watch only $75.00 – 125.00
Scarce box and insert $200.00 – 400.00

Snow White Wristwatch
Date: 1954 • Maker: U.S. Time
Box lid has sketches of Seven Dwarfs with cellophane
oval showing punch-out cardboard figure of Snow White
and watch. Red cloth strap.
Watch only $75.00 – 125.00
Box and insert only $275.00 – 375.00

Snow White Wristwatch
Date: 1950s • Maker: Ingersoll/U.S. Time
Close-up of Snow White wearing yellow
and red outfit. Red vinyl strap.
$75.00 – 125.00

Snow White Wristwatch
Date: 1950s • Maker: Ingersoll/U.S. Time
Close-up of Snow White with yellow
plastic bezel and yellow cloth band.
$75.00 – 125.00

Snow White Wristwatch
Date: 1958 • Maker: U.S. Time
Snow White porcelain statue with cardboard
display stand. "Snow White" only on watch dial.
Watch only $75.00 – 125.00
Display stand and statue only $100.00 – 175.00

Snow White Wristwatch
Date: 1958 • Maker: U.S. Time
Close-up of dial with "Snow White."
$75.00 – 125.00

Snow White Wristwatch
Date: 1958 • Maker: U.S. Time
Plastic statue used to display Snow White watch.
Watch only $80.00 – 130.00
Statue only $45.00 – 65.00

Snow White Wristwatch
Date: 1958 • Maker: U.S. Time
Close-up of Snow White with Dopey. White plastic band.
$80.00 – 130.00

Snow White Toy Watches
Date: 1960s • Maker: Japan
Three styles of different toy watches on colorful
display card. Colored elastic bands. Snow White,
cottage, and Seven Dwarfs shown on display card.
$45.00 – 85.00

Time-Teacher Wristwatch
Date: 1970s • Maker: Sheffield
Close-up of Time-Teacher showing
minute hand with circle. Indicates "past" or "to"
the hour. One jewel movement.
$75.00 – 125.00

Time-Teacher Wristwatch
Date: 1970s • Maker: Sheffield
Close-up of Time-Teacher with
colorful inner workings of watch.
$75.00 – 125.00

Woody Woodpecker Wristwatch
Date: 1950 • Maker: Ingraham
Woody is running saying "Ha Ha Ha."
Rectangular chromium case.
$275.00 – 375.00

Woody Woodpecker Wristwatch
Date: 1950 • Maker: Ingraham
Smaller version of Woody running. Round
chromium case. Blue leather band.
$275.00 – 375.00

Woody Woodpecker Wristwatch
Date: 1971 • Maker: Webster
Woody's little friend is animated at 9:00 position on dial.
$65.00 – 90.00

Comic Pocket Watches

Betty Boop Pocket Watch
Date: 1934 • Maker: Ingraham
Very rare. Betty Boop is pictured with black outfit.
Black garter. Long black gloves act as hour and
minute hand. Less than 10 known to exist.
Complete pocket watch with original face and
embossed back $5,200.00 – 6,700.00

Betty Boop Pocket Watch
Date: 1934 • Maker: Ingraham
Very rare. Original die-embossed back
showing Betty Boop and her dog Bimbo. Stars
and a crescent moon are also engraved on reverse.
Complete pocket watch with original face and
embossed back $5,200.00 – 6,700.00

Big Bad Wolf Pocket Watch
Date: 1934 • Maker: Ingersoll
Scarce. Big Bad Wolf pocket watch has
blinking eye acting as second hand. Three Little
Pigs are also shown. Attached to pocket watch is
enamel fob with Three Little Pigs playing instruments.
Complete pocket watch with original face and
embossed back $800.00 – 1,200.00
Fob only $75.00 – 125.00

Big Bad Wolf Pocket Watch
Date: 1934 • Maker: Ingersoll
Scarce. Back of pocket watch shows brick
wall incised with "May The Big Bad Wolf
Never Come To Your Door/Walt Disney."
Complete pocket watch with original face and
embossed back $800.00 – 1,200.00

Big Bad Wolf Matchbox Holder
Date: 1930s • Maker: Unknown
Green enamel brass matchbox holder with
Three Little Pigs playing instruments singing
"Who's Afraid of the Big Bad Wolf?"
$60.00 – 95.00

Big Bad Wolf Bank
Date: 1930s • Maker: Unknown
Yellow leatherette bank with Three Little
Pigs singing "We Save Our Coins/So Who's
Afraid of the Big Bad Wolf?"
$75.00 – 125.00

Donald Duck Pocket Watch
Date: 1939 • Maker: Ingersoll
Scarce. Pocket watch with Donald Duck in
blue sailor outfit. Back of pocket watch is plain.
Some have decal of Mickey Mouse on back.
Decal was used to increase sales.
$800.00 – 1,300.00

Donald Duck Pocket Watch
Date: 1954 • Maker: Ward W. Co. (Swiss made)
Scarce. Animated Donald Duck hands. Probably
used as lady's lapel watch. Pocket watch is thinner
and lighter. Decorative suede fob strap with rhinestones
attached. Enameled black and gold case.
$350.00 – 650.00

Donald Duck Night Light
Date: 1950s • Maker: General Electric
Head shot of Donald Duck used
as night light. Early plastic.
$40.00 – 75.00

Mickey Mouse Pocket Watch
Date: 1933 • Maker: Ingersoll
Scarce. Side-winder at 3:00 position. Possibly a
prototype or fantasy watch made by Al Horen. Horen
was a collector, dealer, and artist who made these fantasy pocket watches. Mickey's standing with no second
hand animation. © 1933 W.E.D. Prod. is under Ingersoll.
$350.00 – 450.00

Mickey Mouse Pocket Watch
Date: 1933 • Maker: Ingersoll
Scarce. Mickey and Minnie are kissing.
Possibly a prototype or fantasy pocket watch
made by Al Horen. Known as a side-winder at
3:00 position. No second hand animation.
$450.00 – 650.00

Mickey Mouse Pocket Watch
Date: 1933 • Maker: Ingersoll
Scarce. This is the early Mickey Mouse pocket watch
with the longer stem on winder. The second hand at
6:00 position has three Mickey images chasing each other.
The nickel-plated brass fob has Mickey Mouse on it with
black highlights. Original leather fob strap is shown.
Pocket watch only $600.00 – 900.00
Fob only $100.00 – 200.00

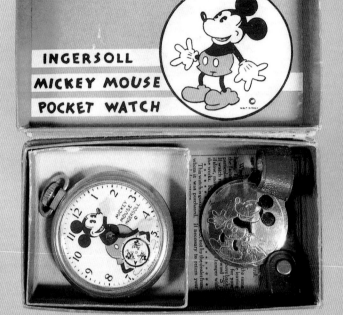

Mickey Mouse Pocket Watch
Date: 1933 • Maker: Ingersoll
Scarce. Close-up of back of pocket watch
shows die-embossed image of Mickey with
words, "Ingersoll/Mickey Mouse."
$600.00 – 900.00

Mickey Mouse Pocket Watch
Date: 1933 • Maker: Ingersoll
Short stem version of Mickey Mouse pocket watch.
Animated second hand with Mickey images at 6:00 posi-
tion. Inside box lid is Mickey in circle. Fob and pocket
watch displayed in original box with papers. Back of
short stem version is same as long stem version.
Pocket watch only $500.00 – 800.00
Box only $175.00 – 300.00
Fob only $100.00 – 200.00

Mickey Mouse Pocket Watch
Date: 1933 • Maker: Ingersoll
Short stem pocket watch in "critter" box.
Inside of lid shows Mickey running and
"Ingersoll Mickey Mouse Pocket Watch."
Pocket watch only $500.00 – 800.00
Box only $150.00 – 275.00
Fob only $100.00 – 200.00

Mickey Mouse Pocket Watch
Date: 1934 • Maker: Ingersoll Ltd. (Great Britain)
Rare. English Mickey Mouse pocket watch
has plain back. High gloss paper face. Mickey
with yellow gloves. Three animated walking
Mickeys at 6:00 position. Military time is on dial.
The word "Foreign" is under the 30/18 position.
Mickey's legs and shoes are smaller than usual.
$800.00 – 1,200.00

Mickey Mouse Pocket Watch
Date: 1934 • Maker: Ingersoll Ltd. (Great Britain)
Rare. English version of Mickey mouse pocket
watch with longer tail. Orange five-fingered gloves.
Larger legs and orange shoes. The famous five
o'clock shadow. Military time on dial. Three walking
Mickeys as second hand. "Foreign" appears below 30/18
position. High gloss paper on dial.
$800.00 – 1,200.00

Mickey Mouse Pin-Back
Date: 1934 • Maker: Ingersoll Ltd. (Great Britain)
Scarce. Original Mickey Mouse button
showing Mickey and "Ingersoll/Mickey Mouse
Watches/Clocks." Mickey's popularity spread
to England creating this advertising pin-back.
$90.00 – 125.00

Mickey Mouse Pocket Watch
Date: 1935 • Maker: Ingersoll
Possibly prototype or Al Horen creation. Three Mickeys
at 6:00 position. Dial is dated 1935 W.D. Prod.
$450.00 – 600.00

Mickey Mouse Pocket Watch
Date: 1934 • Maker: Ingersoll
Most probably made by Al Horen. Al Horen
was a collector, dealer, and artist who made these
fantasy pocket watches. "1934 W.D. Prod." is printed
on dial. Regular second hand at 6:00 position. Al
Horen creations have become very collectible.
$375.00 – 475.00

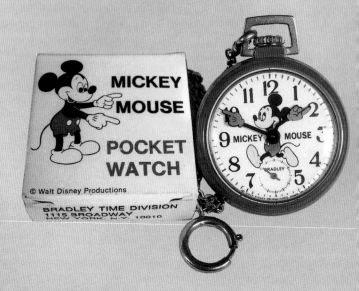

Mickey Mouse Pocket Watch
Date: 1934 • Maker: Ingersoll
Close-up of back of Mickey Mouse pocket
watch. Has waffle-like appearance. Pocket
watch is lighter in weight (typical of Al Horen
creation), possibly made in the 1960s.
$375.00 – 475.00

Mickey Mouse Pocket Watch
Date: 1974 • Maker: Bradley
Came in red plastic case. Second
hand between Mickey's feet.
Pocket watch only $75.00 – 125.00
Box only $25.00 – 50.00

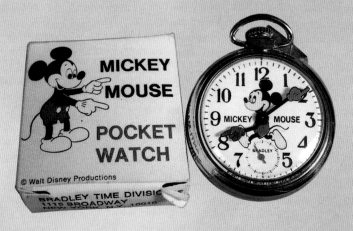

Mickey Mouse Pocket Watch
Date: 1974 • Maker: Bradley
Came in chromium case. Bradley on
seconds dial between Mickey's feet.
Pocket watch only $75.00 – 125.00
Box only $25.00 – 50.00

Moon Mullins Pocket Watch
Date: early 1930s • Maker: Ingersoll
Rare. One of the first comic character pocket
watches. Colorful dial showing Moon Mullins
and Kayo. Artist name Willard is written on dial.
$675.00 – 975.00

Popeye Pocket Watch
Date: 1934 • Maker: New Haven
Rare. Animated hands. At the second hand
position, Wimpy is chasing the elusive hamburger.
Colorful dial with Thimble Theater Players.
$800.00 – 1,200.00

Popeye Pocket Watch
Date: 1935 • Maker: New Haven
Rare. Animated hands and arms.
Popeye shown alone on dial. 1934
model was too crowded and too busy.
$800.00 – 1,200.00

Skeezix Pocket Watch
Date: early 1930s • Maker: Ingraham
Scarce. Seldom seen. Nice image of Skeezix with
"SKEEZIX" in orange. Member of Gasoline Alley family.
$400.00 – 700.00

Snow White Pocket Watch
Date: Unknown • Maker: Smiths
Possibly fantasy or prototype. Resembles
Bayard French Snow White clock.
$200.00 – 400.00

Category 8
Comic Heroes

Batman Wristwatch
Date: 1966 • Maker: Gilbert
Scarce. Hands on dial are bat wings with red
second hand. Plastic molded case in shape of bat.
Watch was made during the Batman TV series.
$275.00 – 400.00

Battlestar Galactica Wristwatch
Date: 1979 • Maker: Bradley
Starship acts as second hand.
$55.00 – 85.00

Buck Rogers Pocket Watch
Date: 1935 • Maker: Ingraham
Rare. Colorful dial shows Buck holding his
rocket gun with Wilma by his side. Copper hands
are in the shape of lighting bolts.
$800.00 – 1,200.00

Buck Rogers Pocket Watch
Date: 1935 • Maker: Ingraham
Rare. Close-up of reverse of pocket watch
with embossed one-eyed Tiger Man.
$800.00 – 1,200.00

Buzz Corey (Space Patrol) Wristwatch
Date: 1952 • Maker: U.S. Time
Dial has white metal background with red
and black numerals. Used as time-teacher with
military time. "Space Patrol" is printed on dial.
$125.00 – 175.00

Captain Marvel Wristwatch
Date: 1948 • Maker: Fawcett Publishing Inc. (Marvel Import)
Large size in round chromium case with red
vinylite band. Colorful box with standup insert.
Watch only $300.00 – 400.00
Box only $200.00 – 350.00

Captain Marvel Wristwatch
Date: 1948 • Maker: Fawcett Publishing Inc. (Marvel Import)
Variation 1. Close-up of Captain Marvel holding
airplane in left hand. Vinylite bands came in blue, red,
and green. Foil price tag $6.95 attached to blue band.
$300.00 – 400.00

Captain Marvel Wristwatch
Date: 1948 • Maker: Fawcett Publishing Inc. (Marvel Import)
Variation 2. Smaller size dial with one jewel
movement. This version cost $1.00 more.
$350.00 – 450.00

Captain Marvel Pocket Watch
Date: 1940s • Maker: Unknown
Scarce. Colorful dial. Possibly a
prototype or fantasy pocket watch.
$400.00 – 700.00

Dan Dare Pocket Watch
Date: 1953 • Maker: Ingersoll Ltd. (Great Britain)
Scarce. English double-animated pocket watch.
Dan Dare's arm moves as he holds space gun. Second
animation shows moving rocket ship at 6:00 position.
This was England's conception of Buck Rogers.
$450.00 – 650.00

Dan Dare Pocket Watch
Date: 1953 • Maker: Ingersoll Ltd. (Great Britain)
Scarce. Close-up of back of pocket watch. Shows engraved eagle with "Eagle" incised below it. This was a
trademark for Eagle Comic Books in Great Britain.
$450.00 – 650.00

Flash Gordon Wristwatch
Date: 1971 • Maker: Precision Time
Rare. Only watch made by Precision Time.
Less than 200 were produced. Colorful dial with
no numerals. Flash pictured holding space gun.
Hands and bezel are gold-toned with blue suede
band. Colorful box with plastic cover. Signature
of artist Gray Morrow appears on box.
Watch only $200.00 – 350.00
Box only $250.00 – 400.00

Mary Marvel Wristwatch
Date: 1948 • Maker: Fawcett Publishing Inc.
Dial shows Mary Marvel in flying position. Small round chromium case with blue vinylite band.
$125.00 – 225.00

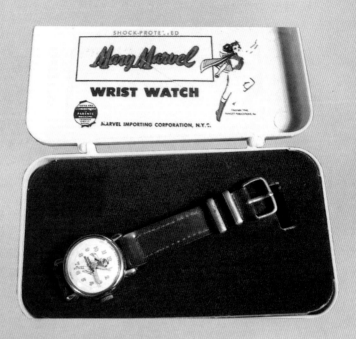

Mary Marvel Wristwatch
Date: 1948 • Maker: Fawcett Publishing Inc.
Scarce. Yellow plastic box. Label inside lid reads "Commended by Parents Magazine." Inside lid has decal of Mary Marvel in flying position.
Watch only $125.00 – 225.00
Box only $275.00 – 375.00

Mighty Mouse Wristwatch
Date: 1981 • Maker: Bradley
Terrytoons character with animated hands, wearing red cape.
$60.00 – 95.00

Rocky Jones Wristwatch
Date: 1954 • Maker: Ingraham
Variation 1. Small rectangular case shows Rocky Jones in front of space ship. Planet, stars, and "Space Ranger" shown on dial. Scarce watch band shows rocket ship encircling planet.
$275.00 – 375.00

Rocky Jones Wristwatch
Date: 1954 • Maker: Ingraham
Variation 2. Larger rectangular case
version is shown with plain band.
$175.00 – 275.00

Space Explorer Wristwatch
Date: 1960s • Maker: Unknown
astronaut and satellite is shown
on dial. Rotating disc acts as
second hand.
$50.00 – 75.00

Superman Wristwatch
Date: 1939 • Maker: New Haven
Scarce. Upper portion of Superman's
body is shown on dial. "Superman"
is printed under his legs. Larger case.
$200.00 – 400.00

Superman Wristwatch
Date: 1948 • Maker: New Haven
Smaller rectangular case compared to 1939 model.
"Superman" is printed across upper legs.
$200.00 – 400.00

Superman Wristwatch
Date: 1948 • Maker: New Haven
Round case has horn-like bezel. Uniquely styled bezel is
similar to Dick Tracy and Little Orphan Annie of 1948.
$225.00 – 425.00

Superman Wristwatch
Date: 1955 • Maker: Bradley
Watch has full figure of Superman. Red lightning bolt
hands. Colorful yellow box with Superman flying on lid.
Watch only $200.00 – 300.00
Box only $175.00 – 275.00

Superman Wristwatch
Date: 1955 • Maker: Bradley
Close-up of Superman shown in full figure.
$200.00 – 300.00

Superman Wristwatch
Date: 1968 • Maker: Bradley
Animated seconds disc. Superman flying on inside
of lid. Round gold-toned case with expansion band.
Watch only $125.00 – 225.00
Box only $75.00 – 125.00.

Superman Wristwatch
Date: 1968 • Maker: Bradley
Close-up of Superman flying on
second hand disc that revolves.
$125.00 – 225.00

Superman Pocket Watch
Date: 1959 • Maker: Bradley
Scarce. Stop watch button located on case
between 10:00 and 11:00 position. Inner circle
indicates hours and outer circle indicates seconds
on stopwatch. Superman is flying over city on dial.
Case is chrome-plated.
$450.00 – 750.00

Superman Pocket Watch
Date: Unknown • Maker: Unknown
Possibly fantasy or foreign import. Gold-toned case.
$50.00 – 85.00

Superman Pocket Watch
Date: Unknown • Maker: Unknown
Waffle-like back. Lighter in weight.
$50.00 – 85.00

Tom Corbett (Space Cadet) Wristwatch
Date: 1951 • Maker: Ingraham
Facial shot of Tom Corbett with space ship on dial.
Decorative watchband showing space ship and planet.
$175.00 – 250.00

Famous Personalities

Spiro Agnew Wristwatch
Date: 1971 • Maker: Dirty Time Co.
Animated peace hands. "D.T.C." printed on dial.
$75.00 – 125.00

Spiro Agnew Wristwatch
Date: 1971 • Maker: Dirty Time Co.
"Dirty Time Company" is printed on dial. Red, white,
and blue fabric wristband. Animated peace hands.
$75.00 – 125.00

Spiro Agnew Wristwatch
Date: 1970s • Maker: E.G.T.C.
"Official Spiro Agnew" watch. Dressed
as Uncle Sam holding U.S. flag.
$75.00 – 125.00

Spiro Agnew Wristwatch
Date: 1970s • Maker: Unknown (Swiss made)
Face appears on dial with printed name
"Spiro." Blue stars show between numerals.
$75.00 –125.00

Spiro Agnew Wristwatch
Date: 1970s • Maker: Unknown
Spiro Agnew seen on dial in full figure
caricature with golf clubs and speaking into
microphone. Peace signs replace some numerals.
Deluxe gold-toned case with fancy bezel.
$100.00 – 200.00

Spiro Agnew Pocket Watch
Date: 1971 • Maker: Dirty Time Co.
Comic figure of Spiro Agnew on dial dressed
in red, white, and blue shorts and shoes.
$100.00 – 200.00

Admiral Byrd Pocket Watch
Date: 1928 • Maker: Ingraham
Scarce. Trail Blazer Commemorative pocket watch.
Obverse shows Admiral Byrd flying over the Antarctic.
Greenish dial with decorative bezel.
$550.00 – 800.00

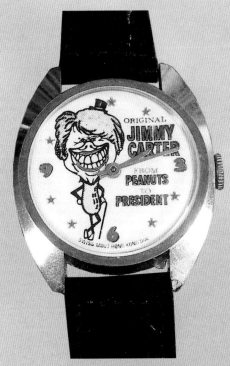

Jimmy Carter Wristwatch
Date: 1976 • Maker: Hong Kong
Caricature of Jimmy Carter saying
"From Peanuts to President."
$65.00 – 95.00

Clark Gable Wristwatch
Date: 1987 • Maker: Harilela Bob Ltd. (Hong Kong)
"King of Hollywood" is written on dial. Watch came in
blister pack from the Memories Movie Star Collection.
$75.00 – 125.00

Clark Gable Wristwatch
Date: 1992 • Maker: Valdawn, Inc. (Hong Kong)
Distributed by Turner Entertainment. Colorful dial
with Rhett Butler embracing Scarlett O'Hara. "Gone
With the Wind" is imprinted on gold-toned bezel.
$100.00 – 200.00

Jerry Lewis Wristwatch
Date: 1971 • Maker: Helbros
Variation 1. Seven jewel movement. Silver
background dial. "Invincible" is printed
above Jerry Lewis's head. Red leatherette
watchband. Came in black plastic hinged box.
Watch only $100.00 – 175.00
Box only $50.00 – 75.00

Jerry Lewis Wristwatch
Date: 1971 • Maker: Helbros
Variation 2. Seven jewel movement calendar watch.
White background on dial. Red-haired caricature of
Jerry Lewis. Came in black plastic hinged box.
Watch only $100.00 – 175.00
Box only $50.00 – 75.00

Charles Lindbergh Pocket Watch
Date: 1928 • Maker: Ingraham
Scarce. Variation 1. Non-stop flight "New York to Paris."
Obverse shows Lindbergh's plane in flight. Background
is off-white with black hands with engraved bezel. Fob
shows Statue of Liberty, Eiffel Tower, and Lindbergh's
plane. Attached to fob is a compass.
Pocket watch only $550.00 – 800.00
Fob only $75.00 – 125.00

Charles Lindbergh Pocket Watch
Date: 1928 • Maker: Ingraham
Scarce. Close-up of reverse shows engraved
scene of New York skyline and Eiffel Tower.
Engraved on wings of plane is "New York to Paris."
$550.00 – 800.00

Charles Lindbergh Pocket Watch
Date: 1928 • Maker: Ingraham
Scarce. Variation 2. Obverse shows black
dial with greenish hands. Engraved back and
fob same as pervious example.
Pocket watch only $550.00 – 800.00
Fob only $75.00 – 125.00

Charles Lindbergh Pocket Watch
Date: Unknown • Maker: Germany
Black and white sketches of plane, clouds,
and Lindbergh in flight jacket. Brass case.
$350.00 – 475.00

Charles Lindbergh Pocket Watch
Date: Unknown • Maker: Unknown
Possibly a fantasy or Al Horen creation.
Portrait photograph of Charles Lindbergh on
obverse, plus Spirit of St. Louis airplane and
two American flags in red, white, and blue.
$125.00 – 175.00

Charles Lindbergh Pocket Watch
Date: Unknown • Maker: Unknown
Reverse has waffle-like surface. Lightweight
pocket watch (typical of Al Horen creations).
$125.00 – 175.00

Lester Maddox Wristwatch
Date: 1971 • Maker: Westclox
Seventeen jewel watch came in red
plastic box. Watch box came in attractive
red, white, and blue wrapper sleeve.
Watch only $75.00 – 125.00
Box and sleeve only $50.00 – 90.00

Lester Maddox Wristwatch
Date: 1971 • Maker: Westclox
Animated chicken bone hands.
Lester Maddox seated on bicycle on dial.
His name replaces numerals on dial.
Watch only $75.00 – 125.00
Box only $35.00 – 65.00

Nixon Wristwatch
Date: 1970s • Maker: E.G.T. (Chateau)
Caricature of Richard Nixon. Red, white, and
blue shield below his head. Gold-toned case.
$75.00 – 125.00

Nixon Wristwatch
Date: 1974 • Maker: All American Time
Printed on dial Nixon says "I'm Not
A Crook." Animated eyes.
$175.00 – 200.00

Queen Elizabeth II Pocket Watch
Date: 1953 • Maker: Ingersoll L.T.D. (Great Britain)
Scarce. Variation 1. Queen Elizabeth II Coronation
pocket watch. The word "Coronation" replaces
numerals on dial. Winder is shown as crown.
Pin-back of Queen Elizabeth is also shown.
Pocket watch only $375.00 – 475.00
Pin-back only $75.00 – 100.00

Queen Elizabeth II Pocket Watch
Date: 1953 • Maker: Ingersoll L.T.D.
English coat-of-arms engraved on reverse.
$375.00 – 475.00

Queen Elizabeth II Pocket Watch
Date: 1953 • Maker: Ingersoll L.T.D.
Scarce. Variation 2. Queen Elizabeth on horse
with riding habit. "Elizabeth II" replaces numerals
on dial. June 2, 1953, date on dial. Winder resembles
crown. English coat-of-arms on reverse. Rhinestone
pin in shape of coronation carriage shown.
Pocket watch only $375.00 – 475.00
Pin only $100.00 – 150.00

Shirley Temple Wristwatch
Date: 1935 • Maker: Unknown
Rare. "Little Colonel" printed on watch dial. Silhouette
of Shirley Temple as the "Little Colonel" in oval at 6:00
position. Watch was probably unauthorized.
$600.00 – 700.00

Shirley Temple Pin
Date: 1935 • Maker: Unknown
Scarce. "Little Colonel" pin. Silhouette of Shirley
Temple in Little Colonel hat. Blue enamel.
$125.00 – 175.00

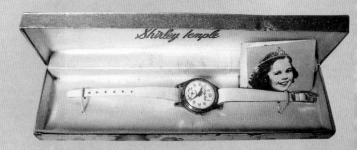

Shirley Temple Pocket Watch
Date: 1953 • Maker: Westclox
Scarce. Photo of Shirley Temple on dial with knees up.
Printed on dial "Shirley Temple Paramount Pictures."
$400.00 – 500.00

Shirley Temple Wristwatch
Date: 1950s • Maker: Swiss Made
Rare. First official Shirley Temple wristwatch.
Her name is written on dial. Came in gold and
blue hinged rectangular box. Photos in booklet
show Shirley Temple with her daughter.
Watch only $400.00 – 500.00
Box and booklet only $75.00 – 100.00

Shirley Temple Wristwatch
Date: 1950s • Maker: Swiss Made
Rare. Close-up of watch with Shirley Temple's name
written on dial. Numbers glow in the dark. Second
hand is at the 6:00 position. White leather band.
$400.00 – 500.00

Shirley Temple Wristwatch
Date: 1950s • Maker: Swiss Made
Shirley Temple's signature on dial.
Gold-toned numbers on gold-toned bezel.
$175.00 – 250.00

Shirley Temple Wristwatch
Date: 1970s • Maker: Unknown
Full shot of Shirley Temple as Little Colonel.
$45.00 – 75.00

Shirley Temple Jewelry
Date: 1930s • Maker: Unknown
Scarce items.
A – Czechoslovakian sterling
silver ring with head shot of Shirley Temple.
$50.00 – 100.00
B – Shirley Temple photo ring on
brass from Czechoslovakia.
$100.00 – 175.00
C – Gold-toned bracelet with head
shot of Shirley Temple in center.
$50.00 – 100.00

Shirley Temple Pin
Date: 1936 • Maker: Unknown
Baby Take A Bow movie pose. Trimmed in silver.
$125.00 – 225.00

Shirley Temple Enamel Pin
Date: 1937 • Maker: Premium (Great Britain)
Scarce. Reads "Sunday Referee/Shirley Temple League."
Possible premium from English newspaper.
$85.00 – 175.00

Shirley Temple Script Pin with Charms
Date: 1930s • Maker: Unknown
Carded script pin with charms including gold-toned heart with "Shirley Temple," enamel Baby Take a Bow charm, and gold-toned bear with green ball.
$100.00 – 175.00

Shirley Temple Metal Photo Box
Date: 1930s • Maker: Czechoslovakia
Rare. Highly decorated miniature box with Shirley Temple photo on lid. Box contains seven photos of Shirley from movies.
$400.00 – 500.00

Silent Majority Wristwatch
Date: 1970 • Maker: Unknown (Swiss)
Richard Nixon in favor of the Vietnam War. Majority of Americans were silent on the issue. Red, white, and blue wristband.
$75.00 – 125.00

Uncle Sam Pocket Watch
Date: 1940s • Maker: Ingraham
Patriotic pocket watch with fob showing 13 stars. Dial is silver metallic with copper metallic numbers. "Uncle Sam" is printed on dial.
Pocket watch only $125.00 – 175.00
Fob only $50.00 – 75.00

Uncle Sam Pocket Watch
Date: 1940s • Maker: Ingersoll
Uncle Sam and airplane are on metallic
dial. Second hand is located at 6:00 position.
$125.00 – 175.00

Uncle Sam Wristwatch
Date: 1972 • Maker: Swiss Made
Uncle Sam calendar watch with red sweep second
hand. The word "Vote" is printed on his chest.
$50.00 – 75.00

George Washington Pocket Watch
Date: 1932 • Maker: Ingraham
Scarce. Commemorates George Washington as "The
Patriot." Celebrates his 200th birthday. Small portrait
of George Washington and "The Patriot" printed on dial.
Large brass fob with portrait of George Washington,
date 1732 – 1932, and his name engraved on fob.
Pocket watch only $275.00 – 400.00
Fob only $150.00 – 225.00

George Washington Pocket Watch
Date: 1932 • Maker: Ingraham
Scarce. Reverse of Patriot pocket watch. Engraving
of George Washington, also shown are engraved
words "Patriot," "George Washington," "Bicentennial,"
date "1732 – 1932." Reverse of fob has "George Washington Bicentennial Membership Campaign/JP/O.U.A.M."
Pocket watch only $275.00 – 400.00
Fob only $150.00 – 225.00

Zep Pocket Watch
Date: 1929 • Maker: Westclox
Variation 1. Black background on dial. Hands
and numerals glow in the dark. Silver-toned case.
$400.00 – 550.00

Zep Pocket Watch
Date: 1929 • Maker: Westclox
Reverse of silver-toned case. Shows
Graf Zeppelin and Magellan's ship. Engraved
on back is the word "Trailblazer."
$400.00 – 550.00

Zep Pocket Watch
Date: 1929 • Maker: Westclox
Variation 2. White background on dial with black
numerals and hands. Gold-toned case. Attached is
fob engraved with plane, ship, and dirigible.
Pocket watch only $400.00 – 550.00
Fob only $75.00 – 125.00

Zep Pocket Watch
Date: 1929 • Maker: Westclox
Reverse of gold-toned case or brass case.
Has engraving comparing Graf Zeppelin to
Magellan's voyage around the world.
$400.00 – 550.00

Advertising Heartbeat Clock
Date: 1930s • Maker: Lux Clock Co.
Scarce. "Commonwealth" replaces numbers on dial.
"Commonwealth Life" is printed on dial. Clock is mount-
ed in wooden case. Eight sided dial with beveled glass.
$150.00 – 225.00

Arch-shaped Heartbeat Clock
Date: 1930s • Maker: Lux Clock Co.
Typical Art Deco brass rim. Two small pearls
at top. Black pinstripe on yellow celluloid
case. "Heartbeat" printed on dial.
$150.00 – 200.00

Beehive-shaped Heartbeat Clock
Date: 1920s • Maker: Germany
Large white onyx heartbeat clock with
rose-colored veining. Gold-toned dial and trim.
$125.00 – 175.00

Beehive-shaped Heartbeat Clock
Date: 1920s • Maker: Germany
White ceramic heartbeat clock with flowers
on case. Gold-toned dial and trim.
$125.00 – 175.00

Butterfly-shaped Heartbeat Clock
Date: 1930s • Maker: Schorcos (France)
Red bakelite case. Gold-toned metallic
dial with copper-toned hands.
$125.00 – 175.00

Cathedral-shaped Heartbeat Clock
Date: 1920s • Maker: Germany
Peach colored bakelite case. Gold-toned metallic dial.
$165.00 – 225.00

Cathedral Radio-shaped Heartbeat Clock
Date: 1930s • Maker: Lux Clock Co.
Three small yellow rhinestones on cream
colored celluloid case. Black pinstriping.
$165.00 – 225.00

Crown-shaped Heartbeat Clock
Date: 1930s • Maker: Lux Clock Co. (Swiss)
Scarce. Fleur de lis miniature heartbeat clock. Fancy bezel with mother-of-pearl on gold-toned case. Top of case resembles gold-toned crown. Fancy engraved back.
$150.00 – 225.00

Curve-shaped Heartbeat Clock
Date: 1930s • Maker: Lux Clock Co.
Four rhinestones on hand-painted flowers.
Pearl-like celluloid case. "Heartbeat" printed on dial.
$150.00 – 225.00

Dome-shaped Heartbeat Clock
Date: 1920s • Maker: Germany
Country scene painted on delft case.
Gold-toned beaded edge.
$250.00 – 325.00

Dome-shaped Heartbeat Clock
Date: 1930s • Maker: Lux Clock Co.
Pearl-like bakelite case with hand-painted blue flowers.
$150.00 – 200.00

Geometric Heartbeat Clock
Date: 1920s • Maker: Germany
Large ceramic heartbeat clock with gold pinstriping.
Gold-toned dial and rim. Makers mark on reverse.
$175.00 – 225.00

Grandfather Clock-shaped Heartbeat Clock
Date: c. 1940 • Maker: Kronheimer Co., Inc.
Heartbeat clock movement inside wooden
grandfather-type case. Gold-toned fancy dial.
$75.00 – 125.00

Heart-shaped Heartbeat Clock
Date: 1930s • Maker: Lux Clock Co.
Gold- and silver-toned metal dial. Trademark,
"Heartbeat" written on dial. Bakelite
heart-shaped case. Pearl-like color.
$125.00 – 175.00

Hexagonal Heartbeat Clock
Date: 1920s • Maker: Germany
White onyx case attached to onyx base.
Gold-toned dial and rim. Larger than most Heartbeats.
$75.00 – 125.00

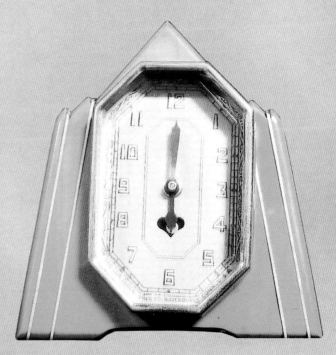

Mountain-shaped Heartbeat Clock
Date: 1930s • Maker: Lux Clock Co.
Dark blue bakelite case. Typical Art Deco
rim around dial. "Heartbeat" trademark printed
on silver- and gold-toned dial.
$140.00 – 200.00

Pyramid-shaped Heartbeat Clock
Date: 1930s • Maker: Lux Clock Co.
Depression green Art Deco bakelite case.
Eight sided dial. Beveled glass.
$140.00 – 200.00

Syrocco Case Heartbeat Clock
Date: 1930s • Maker: Lux Clock Co.
Yellow, light green, and rose colored pressed
wood case (Syrocco). Art Deco rim around dial.
"Heartbeat" trademark printed on silver- and
gold-toned dial. Fancy case with flower and vines.
$150.00 – 200.00

Syrocco Case Heartbeat Clock
Date: 1930s • Maker: Lux Clock Co.
Large sized deluxe clock with typical Art Deco
rim around dial. "Heartbeat" trademark on dial.
Brown Syrocco (pressed wood) in square
case. Fancy designs on all four corners.
$150.00 – 200.00

Novelty and Pendulette Clocks

Blind Man Pocket Watch
Date: 1930s • Maker: Ingersoll
Extended winder at 12:00 position. Crystal
removed with metal hands elevated.
$125.00 – 175.00

Birdcage Alarm Clock
Date: 1930s • Maker: Kaiser (Germany)
Scarce. Animated bird sways back and forth. Brass cage
and stand. Alarm located on bottom of cage. Two silver
rotary dials inside cage, indicate hours and minutes.
$150.00 – 250.00

"God Bless America" Clock
Date: 1940s • Maker: Unknown (Premium)
Premium known as Kate Smith clock. Moving
flag waves at top of metal case. U.S. map and
Statue of Liberty show on face.
$125.00 – 175.00

God Bless America Punchboard
Date: 1940s • Maker: Unknown (Premium)
Twenty names punch out to determine winner
of flag waving electric clock. Colorful card.
Double-sided punchboard only $50.00 – 75.00

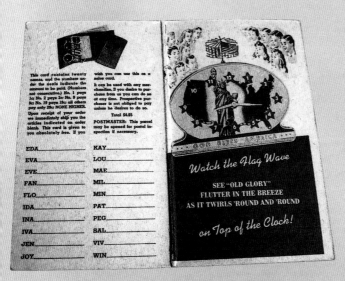

God Bless America Punchboard
Date: 1940s • Maker: Unknown (Premium)
Reverse of card. Has twenty names
to be filled out for flag waving clock.
Double-sided punchboard only $50.00 – 75.00

Lamp Post Clock
Date: 1950s • Maker: Le Coultre (Swiss)
Brass with black enamel. Roman numerals
on clock dial. Clock located between street
light and street sign "Rue De La Paix."
$75.00 – 125.00

Pastor Stop Watch
Date: 1930s • Maker: Sterling Watch Co.
Scarce. Unique pocket watch having paper
face and blue numbers. When stop button is
pressed first time stopwatch hands begin to
move, pressing button second time causes stopwatch
hand to stop, pressing button third time
causes stopwatch hand to fly back to 12:00 position.
Outer numbers used for stopwatch reading.
$350.00 – 450.00

Rotary Tape Measure Clock
Date: 1935 • Maker: Lux Clock Co.
Time pointer attached to fixed metal base
with brass trim. Tape measure rotates. Time is
read by pointer location on tape measure.
$75.00 – 125.00

Rotary Tape Measure Clock
Date: 1935 • Maker: Lux Clock Co.
Scarce. Miniature version of tape measure clock.
Depression green case with brass trim. Tape
measure rotates indicating time by fixed arrow.
$275.00 – 375.00

Tape Measure (clock-type dial)
Date: 1920s • Maker: Germany
Scarce. Miniature bakelite case resembling mantel
clock. Dial shows regular time in black and military
time in red. Cloth tape measure inside case.
$150.00 – 225.00

Savings Bank Alarm Clock
Date: 1890s • Maker: Ansonia Clock Co.
Rare. Paper dial with Roman numerals. Alarm set dial
under 12:00 position. Black metal case. Penny drop
located near alarm bell on nickel-plated case. Inserting
penny releases ratchet allowing clock to be wound.
Penny drops into combination safe. Used as bank.
$700.00 – 900.00

Savings Bank Clock
Date: 1925 • Maker: Lux Clock Co.
Dime or quarter inserted in slot to wind
the clock. Lever on back releases coin into bank.
Has key to open bank. Possibly used as premium.
$175.00 – 275.00

Tank Clock
Date: 1920s • Maker: Germany
Two German tanks on mountainous terrain. Heavy
metal clock with gold-toned trim around dial.
$150.00 – 250.00

War Alarm Clock
Date: 1943 • Maker: LaSalle
Lightweight pressed fiberboard. "War Alarm"
printed on dial. Also "La Salle, IL." Sold for $1.65.
Embargo on metal created fiberboard clock.
$125.00 – 175.00

Pendulette Clocks

Brown Cat Pendulette Clock
Date: 1933 • Maker: Lux Clock Co.
Animated eyes move as pendulum tail
swings back and forth. Made of Syrocco
(pressed wood). Available in black, white, or
brown. Hung on wall or Lux Syrocco stand.
$175.00 – 275.00

Clown Pendulette Clock
Date: 1937 • Maker: Lux Clock Co.
Ball moves from one seal to another seal as
pendulum moves. Colorful clown clock. Made of
painted Syrocco (pressed wood). Usually hung on wall.
$200.00 – 300.00

Sally Rand Pendulette Clock
Date: 1933 • Maker: Lux Clock Co.
Clock modeled after the famous fan
dancer, Sally Rand. Pendulum moves
causing feathered fan to move back
and forth. Displays nicely when hung
from Lux Syrocco stand.
$375.00 – 475.00

Sally Rand Clock Box
Date: 1933 • Maker: Lux Clock Co.
Animated fan dancer clock #335.
Guarantee on front and how to
regulate the clock. Sold at Century
of Progress in Chicago.
$50.00 – 100.00

Shmoo Pendulette Clock
Date: 1948 • Maker: Lux Clock Co.
Created by Al Capp in
the Li'l Abner comic strip.
Lovable character that "That tried
to make people happy." Came
in white, blue, or pink.
$300.00 – 400.00

Shmoo Pendulette Clock Box
Date: 1948 • Maker: Lux Clock Co.
Colorful box showing Li'l Abner and
Shmoo being chased by Daisy Mae. Dog
Patch players shown on sides of box.
$150.00 – 250.00

Woody Woodpecker Pendulette Clock
Date: 1959 • Maker: Columbia Time
Woody dressed as cowboy. Has moving
spur and stirrup. Created by Walter Lantz.
$200.00 – 300.00

Scouting

Boy Scouts

Boy Scout Wristwatch Box
Date: 1937 • Maker: Ingersoll
Scarce. Hinged box with Boy Scout
emblem with brown and orange colors.
Box only $300.00 – 425.00

Boy Scout Wristwatch
Date: 1937 • Maker: Ingersoll
Scarce. Variation 1. Printed on yellow hour hand
"Be Prepared." Yellow minute hand says "A Scout Is."
Scout code is printed on outer dial, which includes
being Trustworthy, Loyal, Helpful, Friendly, Courteous,
Kind, Obedient, Cheerful, Thrifty, Brave, Clean, and
Reverent. Pictured on dial is a camping scene. Second
hand is moving B.S. emblem. Black leather band.
Watch only $350.00 – 450.00

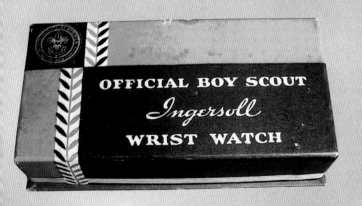

Boy Scout Watch Box
Date: 1937 • Maker: Ingersoll
Scarce. Same as previous Boy Scout box.
$300.00 – 425.00

Boy Scout Wristwatch
Date: 1937 • Maker: Ingersoll
Scarce. Variation 2. Same as variation 1
except B.S. emblem is not on second hand.
Link wristband. Original Ingersoll paper price tag.
Watch only $325.00 – 425.00
Tag only $20.00 – 35.00

Scouting

Boy Scout Wristwatch
Date: 1937 • Maker: Ingersoll
Variation 3. Same as variation 1 except
"Be Prepared" hands not used.
$325.00 – 425.00

Boy Scout Wristwatch
Date: 1938 • Maker: New Haven
Variation 1. "Be Prepared" emblem on center of
dial. Chromium case with metal dial. "B.S.A./National
Council New York City" printed on dial. "Pat's Pend'g"
"New Haven, USA" printed above 12:00 position.
$150.00 – 250.00

Boy Scout Wristwatch
Date: 1938 • Maker: New Haven
Variation 2. Same as variation 1 except "Pat's
Pend'g" and "New Haven, USA" omitted on dial.
$150.00 – 250.00

Boy Scout Wristwatch
Date: 1938 • Maker: New Haven
Variation 3. Same as variation 1 except has early
plastic see-through wristband with decorative rivets.
$150.00 – 250.00

144

Boy Scout Wristwatch
Date: 1940s • Maker: Kelton
Scarce. B.S. emblem located at the 6:00 position
on dial. Red sweep second hand. Glow in the dark
hands and numbers. Shows maritime hours.
$175.00 – 275.00

Boy Scout Wristwatch
Date: 1940s • Maker: Elgin
Scarce. Hexagonal stainless steel case. B.S.
emblem on center of dial. "Boy Scouts of
America"/"Headquarters" "New York City" printed
around emblem. Radium hands and numbers.
"Official Boy Scout" watch incised on bezel. Fancy
engraving at 6:00 and 12:00 on bezel. Link wristband.
$300.00 – 450.00

Boy Scout Wristwatch
Date: 1940s • Maker: Elgin
Scarce. Variation 1. Round gold-toned case. Seven jewels. "Boy Scouts of America" printed under 12:00 position. B.S. emblem below printed words. "Elgin" is printed
above 6:00 position. Gold-toned expansion band.
$275.00 – 400.00

Boy Scout Wristwatch
Date: 1940s • Maker: Elgin
Scarce. Variation 2. Same as variation 1
except has gold-toned second hand. Case
is stainless steel. Black leather band.
$175.00 – 275.00

Boy Scout Wristwatch
Date: 1940s • Maker: Elgin (Canada)
Scarce. "Official Watch/Boy Scouts of Canada"
printed on dial. "Boy Scout" printed on emblem
instead of "Be Prepare." Fancy designs engraved
on four corners of bezel including the four lugs.
$275.00 – 375.00

Boy Scout Wristwatch
Date: 1960s • Maker: Timex
Chromium and stainless steel case.
Silver colored hands and dial. Sweep second
hand. B.S. emblem above 6:00 position.
$85.00 – 125.00

Boy Scout Wristwatch
Date: 1977 • Maker: Timex
Red background on large dial with white numbers.
B.S. emblem beneath 12:00 position. "Scouting/USA"
printed in white letters on dial. Calendar window.
Black sweep second hand. Expansion band.
$85.00 – 125.00

Explorer Wristwatch
Date: 1960s • Maker: Timex
Chromium case. B.S. Explorer emblem
located above 6:00 position. Shiny brownish dial.
Brown leather snap-on wristband.
$85.00 – 125.00

Junior Flyer Wristwatch (Air Scouts)
Date: 1940s • Maker: Elgin
Scarce. Ornate engraved bezel. Propeller sketch on center of dial. "Junior Flyer" printed on dial. Radium B.S. emblem used in place of numbers. Link wristband.
$375.00 – 475.00

Boy's Timekeeper Pocket Watch
Date: c. 1907 • Maker: Unknown
Scarce. "Boy's Timekeeper/$2.50" printed in black on paper dial. Roman numerals on dial. Second hand at 6:00 position. Hinged back with winder inside. Possibly used for early Scouting.
$350.00 – 450.00

Boy Scout Lapel/Pocket Watch
Date: 1930s • Maker: Gruen
Scarce. Ultra-thin nickel-plated lapel watch. Gold-toned numerals and second hand at 6:00 position. Boy Scout tending fire engraved on back. Also rifle, fly fishing rod, geese, trees, and squirrel. Fancy engraved bezel edge. B.S. gold-filled pin attached to lapel or pocket watch.
Lapel watch only $300.00 – 475.00
B. S. pin $50.00 – 75.00

Boy Scout Pocket Watch
Date: 1937 • Maker: Ingersoll
Rare. Variation 1. Camp scene on face of dial. "Be Prepared" on yellow hour hand. "A Scout is" on minute hand. B.S. emblem revolving at second hand. Scout code printed on dial, which includes being Trustworthy, Loyal, Helpful, Friendly, Courteous, Kind, Obedient, Cheerful, Thrifty, Brave, Clean, and Reverent. Gold-toned fob attached to leather strap. B.S. emblem in center of fob. Obverse reads "B.S.A./First Class Scout." Printed on reverse "Boy Scouts of America/Do A Good Turn Daily."
Pocket watch only $600.00 – 800.00
Fob only $100.00 – 150.00

Boy Scout Pocket Watch
Date: 1940s • Maker: Ingersoll
Scarce. Variation 2. Same as variation 1 except
radium hour and minute hands. Plain second
hand. Original Ingersoll price tag.
Pocket watch only $500.00 – 700.00
Tag only $20.00 – 35.00

Boy Scout Jamboree Pocket Watch
Date: 1950s • Maker: Smith's (Great Britain)
Scarce. Animated Scout Master moves arm. Scouts sing-
ing along around campfire. Radium hands and numbers.
$275.00 – 375.00

Boy Scout Pocket Watch
Date: 1950s • Maker: Unknown
Nickel-plated case. Two signal flags in red and blue. Sec-
ond hand at 6:00 position. Time-teacher in red numbers.
$175.00 – 275.00

Boy Scout Pocket Watch
Date: 1950s • Maker: Unknown
Boy Scout holding signal flag incised on reverse.
$175.00 – 275.00

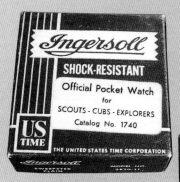

Boy Scout Pocket Watch
Date: 1940s • Maker: Westclox
Chromium case with silvery dial. B.S. emblem
on center of dial. Printed on dial "Boy Scouts
of America/National Council."
$75.00 – 100.00

Boy Scout Pocket Watch
Date: 1950 • Maker: Ingersoll/U.S. Time
Chromium case with silvery dial. "Ingersoll
Sweepster" printed on dial. Red sweep second
hand. B.S. emblem above 6:00 position. Box
reads "Official Pocket Watch for Boy Scouts-Cubs-
Explorers." Box includes receipt and warranty.
Pocket watch only $125.00 – 200.00
Papers only $40.00 – 80.00

Boy Scout Pocket Watch
Date: 1950 • Maker: Unknown
Black and white paper dial showing sketch of Boy Scout
saluting. "Be Prepared" written on ribbon. Radium hands
with red sweep second hand. Chromium case.
$150.00 – 225.00

Boy Scout Pocket Watch
Date: 1960s • Maker: Unknown
Most probably made by Al Horen. Al Horen was a collector, dealer, and artist who made these fantasy pocket
watches. Al Horen creations have become very collectible. Three Scouts are shown on colorful dial.
$100.00 – 175.00

Boy Scout Pocket Watch
Date: 1960s • Maker: Unknown
Close-up of back of pocket watch. Has
waffle-like appearance. Pocket watch is lighter
in weight (typical of Al Horen creations).
$100.00 – 175.00

Boy Scout Pocket Watch
Date: 1960s • Maker: Unknown
Most probably made by Al Horen. Al Horen was a collector, dealer, and artist who made these fantasy pocket
watches. Al Horen creations have become very collectible. Two Scouts on colorful dial holding binoculars and
two signal flags. Printed on dial in black "6th Annual/
Boy Scout Meet, Schuylkill County/September 3 1923."
Waffle-like back same as previous photo. Light weight
typical of Al Horen creations.
$100.00 – 175.00

Boy Scout Compass Watch
Date: 1930s • Maker: Unknown
Nickel-plated case. "Scouts Compass Watch" printed
on paper dial. Second hand at 6:00 position.
$225.00 – 300.00

Boy Scout Compass Watch
Date: 1930s • Maker: Unknown
Small compass on center of reverse.
$225.00 – 300.00

Boy Scout Compass
Date: 1920s • Maker: Waltham
Lid opens showing compass.
Dial of compass made of tin.
$125.00 – 175.00

Boy Scout Compass
Date: 1920s • Maker: Waltham
Embossed B.S. emblem shows on top of lid.
$125.00 – 175.00

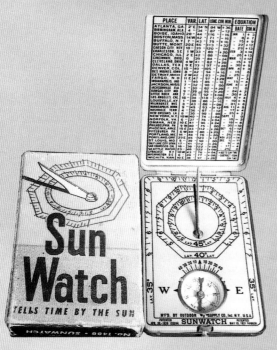

Boy Scout Sun Watch
Date: 1920 • Maker: Outdoor Supply Co.
Gold-toned hinged case houses compass, pointer,
and sundial. Latitude and longitude tables printed
inside lid. Comes in handsome box.
Sun watch only $75.00 – 125.00
Box only $50.00 – 75.00

Boy Scout Hikemeter
Date: c. 1930 • Maker: Unknown
Scarce. Nickel-plated case with belt hanger. Dial
on obverse shows large numbers from 1 to 10 miles.
Second hand measures 10 mile increments. Weight
driven hikemeter calculates distance walked.
$275.00 – 375.00

Boy Scout Hikemeter
Date: c. 1930 • Maker: Unknown
Scarce. Reverse shows B.S. emblem
and compass. Nickel-plated case.
$275.00 – 375.00

Sea Scout Pocket Watch
Date: 1938 • Maker: Nautical Clock Co.
Tells standard and nautical time. Center of dial
shows ship with Seven Seas trademark. Shown
on inner circle are seven watches. "First Dog,
Second Dog, Forenoon Watch, Afternoon Watch,
Morning Watch, First Watch, Mid Watch." Black
and white paper dial. Nickel-plated case.
$100.00 – 150.00

Boy Scout Fob/Medallion
Date: 1910 • Maker: Excelsior Shoe Co.
Obverse shows Boy Scout on horse.
"The Original 'Boy Scout' Shoe for Boys"
printed on medallion/fob, also "July 1910."
$75.00 – 125.00

Boy Scout Fob/Medallion
Date: 1910 • Maker: Excelsior
Trademark embossed on reverse. "Manufactured by Ex-
celsior Shoe Co./Portsmouth, O." embossed near edge.
$75.00 – 125.00

Boy Scout Fob
Date: c. 1920 • Maker: Unknown
Embossed Boy Scout in uniform saluting flag on front of
fob. "Salute the Flag"/"Boy Scout" printed on front of fob.
$60.00 – 100.00

Boy Scout Fob
Date: 1920s • Maker: Unknown
Bugle Boy embossed on brass. Stars adorn surface.
"Boy Scout" engraved on bottom edge.
$50.00 – 90.00

Boy Scout Fob
Date: 1920s • Maker: Unknown
Embossed bust of Boy Scout with crossed rifles and
bugle. "Boy Scout" engraved on top edge.
$50.00 – 90.00

Boy Scout Fob
Date: 1930s • Maker: Unknown
Close-up of Boy Scout near camping tent.
Appears to be nickel-plated.
$40.00 – 75.00

Boy Scout Fob/Medallion
Date: 1930s • Maker: Unknown
Sterling silver fob/medallion, engraved on surface "Black
Hawk Trail Hike/Camp Lowden." Boy Scout emblem
and Black Hawk Indian also embossed on medal.
$75.00 – 125.00

Boy Scout Pin-Back
Date: 1940s • Maker: Offset Gravure Corporation
Close-up of Boy Scout smiling
on red/white/blue background.
$20.00 – 35.00

Cub Scout Wristwatch
Date: 1950s • Maker: U.S. Time/Timex
"Sportster" wristwatch. Cub Scout emblem
above 6:00 position. Time-teacher feature.
$85.00 – 135.00

Cub Scout Wristwatch
Date: c. 1960 • Maker: Timex
Large chromium-plated bezel. Gold-toned hands
and numerals. Gold-toned Cub Scout emblem
above 6:00 position. Time teacher feature.
$75.00 – 100.00

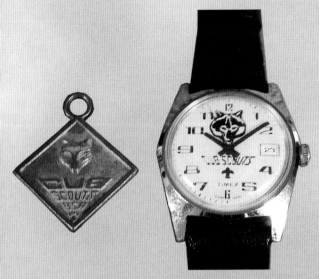

Cub Scout Wristwatch
Date: 1977 • Maker: Timex
Calendar wristwatch with sweep second hand. Black
and yellow wolf cub on dial, Cub Scout medallion with
embossed wolf cub. "Cub Scout/BSA" with paw print on
obverse. Cub Scout pledge engraved on reverse.
Watch only $60.00 – 95.00
Medallion only $25.00 – 50.00

Girl Scout Wristwatch
Date: 1941 • Maker: Ingersoll
Scarce. Rectangular chromium case. G.S. emblem on
center of dial. Red seconds numbers appear in circle
under regular numbers. Red sweep second hand.
$200.00 – 300.00

Girl Scout Wristwatch
Date: 1947 • Maker: Guilford
Rectangular chromium case. Seven jewels. G.S.
emblem in green at 6:00 position. "Girl Scout" printed in
gold on black plastic case. Brown leather band.
Watch only $175.00 – 275.00
Box only $75.00 – 150.00

Girl Scout Wristwatch
Date: 1947 • Maker: Guilford
Box insert says "American Made" with Statue of
Liberty in gold. Green early plastic hinged lid.
Watch only $175.00 – 275.00
Box only $75.00 – 150.00

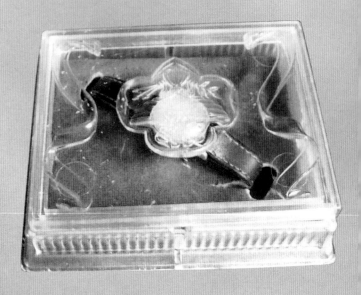

Girl Scout Wristwatch
Date: 1950 • Maker: Medana
Small round bubble-top crystal. Gold-toned hands and numbers. Green and gold-toned G.S. emblem below 12:00 position on dial. Gold-toned second hand located at 6:00 position. Gray strap.
$100.00 – 200.00

Girl Scout Wristwatch
Date: 1950 • Maker: Medana
G.S. emblem embossed on clear early plastic box. Red insert holds watch.
Watch only $100.00 – 200.00
Box only $60.00 – 100.00

Girl Scout Wristwatch
Date: 1957 • Maker: Timex
Gold-toned bezel, hands, numbers, and G.S. emblem. Gold-toned sweep second hand. Black leather band.
$75.00 – 150.00

Girl Scout Wristwatch
Date: 1963 • Maker: Timex
Petite squared chromium case. Silver-colored hands and numbers. G.S. emblem above 6:00 position. Silver-colored expansion band.
$75.00 – 150.00

Girl Scout Wristwatch
Date: 1973 • Maker: Timex
White dial with green hands and numbers.
G.S. emblem and green sweep second hand.
Calendar window on dial. Green leather band.
$75.00 – 125.00

Girl Scout Compass
Date: 1920s • Maker: Unknown
Nickel-plated Girl Scout compass resembling
pocket watch. Printed on center of dial G.S.
emblem "Trademark, Taylor/Rochester, N.Y."
$150.00 – 250.00

Camp Fire Girls

Girl Scout Ring
Date: 1930s • Maker: Unknown
Sterling silver adjustable ring with G.S.
emblem in center.
$75.00 – 125.00

Camp Fire Girls Wristwatch
Date: c. 1955 • Maker: U.S. Time/Timex
Gold-toned bezel, hands, numbers, and sweep second
hand. Gold-toned Camp Fire Girls emblem above 6:00
position. Brown suede wristband made in Italy.
$125.00 – 200.00

RETAIL

F - 111
CAMP FIRE
WRIST WATCH
CHARM

Camp Fire Girls Charm
Date: c. 1955 • Maker: Unknown
"Camp Fire Girls" in silver on blue enamel. Brownish-
orange Camp Fire emblem. Charm on original card.
$65.00 – 100.00

Brownie Scout Wristwatch
Date: c. 1955 • Maker: U.S. Time/Timex
Variation 1. Chromium-plated bezel with gold-toned
hands, numerals, and sweep hand, Brownie
emblem at 6:00 position. "Brownie Scout Watch"
imprinted in gold on red leatherette box lid.
Watch only $75.00 – 125.00
Box only $75.00 – 125.00

Brownie Scout Wristwatch
Date: c. 1955 • Maker: U.S. Time/Timex
Close-up of Brownie wristwatch. Brownie jumping
at 6:00 position. Red leather wristband.
$75.00 – 125.00

Brownie Scout Wristwatch
Date: c. 1960 • Maker: Timex
Variation 2. Raised gold-toned numerals,
hands, and sweep second hand. Gold-toned
Brownie emblem instead of brown colored emblem.
Expansion band instead of leather band.
$75.00 – 125.00

Category 13
Sports

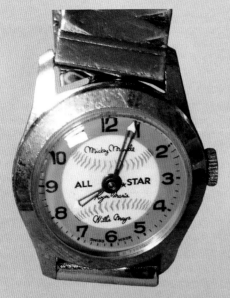

All-Star Baseball Wristwatch
Date: 1966 • Maker: Unknown (Swiss)
Facsimile signatures of Mickey Mantle, Roger Maris,
and Willie Mays on scarce green dial. Expansion band.
$250.00 – 350.00

Babe Ruth Wristwatch
Date: 1930s • Maker: Unknown (U.S.A.)
Rare. Facsimile of Babe Ruth's signature.
Fancy silver-toned bezel.
$400.00 – 600.00

Babe Ruth Wristwatch
Date: 1949 • Maker: Exacta Time
Scarce. Variation 1. Hands and numbers
glow in the dark. Dial shows Babe Ruth
holding two bats. Expansion band.
$450.00 – 650.00

Babe Ruth Wristwatch
Date: 1949 • Maker: Exacta Time
Rare. Variation 2. Watch displayed in early plastic
baseball. Attached to maroon leatherette insert.
Watch only $550.00 – 750.00
Baseball only $375.00 – 475.00

Babe Ruth Wristwatch
Date: 1949 • Maker: Exacta Time
Rare. Variation 2. Green leatherette band with
green dial. Glow-in-the-dark hands and numbers.
$550.00 – 750.00

"Dizzy" Dean Wristwatch
Date: 1935 • Maker: Everbrite Watch Co.
Rare. First baseball player watch. Full figure of "Dizzy"
Dean painted on tin dial. Second hand at 6:00 position.
$500.00 – 700.00

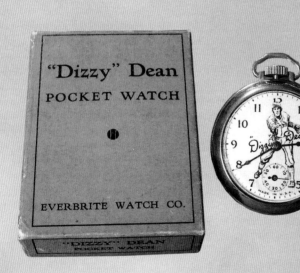

"Dizzy" Dean Pocket Watch
Date: 1935 • Maker: Everbrite Watch Co.
Rare. Paper dial with second hand at 6:00 position.
"Dizzy" Dean in pitching position on dial. First baseball
player pocket watch made. Plain orange box.
Pocket watch only $500.00 – 700.00
Box only $200.00 – 300.00

"Dizzy" Dean Jewelry
Date: 1935 • Maker: Unknown
Three brass "Dizzy" Dean winners
items. Badge, pin, and ring.
Badge only $20.00 – 40.00
Bat pin $50.00 – 80.00
Ring $200.00 – 300.00

Footballer (Soccer) Pocket Watch
Date: 1930s • Maker: Ingersoll L.T.D. (Great Britain)
Colorful animated footballer or soccer player moving left leg. Goalie shown on dial as well. Painted metal dial with second hand at 6:00 position. Greenish box showing footballer kicking soccer ball.
Pocket watch only $275.00 – 375.00
Box only $100.00 – 150.00

Foot Ball Timer Pocket Watch
Date: 1930s • Maker: New Haven
"True Time Teller/Foot Ball Timer" and "start" is written on face of dial. Used as stopwatch. Stop button located on rim. Five minute intervals shown on dial.
$100.00 – 150.00

Football Wristwatch
Date: 1972 • Maker: Webster
Winder at 2:00 position. Animated arm at 10:00 position. Gold-toned rim.
$75.00 – 100.00

Football Wristwatch
Date: 1974 • Maker: Webster
Larger version with animated football at 7:00 position. Gold-toned rim.
$100.00 – 135.00

Hurdle Jumping Toy Pocket Watch
Date: 1930s • Maker: Germany
Three men jumping hurdles. Realistic looking
toy pocket watch. Attached metal chain.
$75.00 – 125.00

Junior League Wristwatch
Date: 1956 • Maker: Ingraham (Bradley)
Junior league baseball player on face of dial.
Companion piece to junior nurse wristwatch.
$100.00 – 150.00

Soccer Wristwatch
Date: 1974 • Maker: Webster
Soccer ball moves at 7:00 position. Two
soccer players shown on dial. Gold-toned rim.
$100.00 – 135.00

Category 14
Western

Annie Oakley

Annie Oakley Wristwatch
Date: 1951 • Maker: Muros Watch Factory
Variation 1. Profile shot of Annie with animated
western gun. Western style watch band and buckle.
$250.00 – 350.00

Annie Oakley Wristwatch
Date: 1951 • Maker: Muros Watch Factory
Variation 2. Smaller case with gold-toned bezel.
Black vinylite band. Animated western gun.
$225.00 – 325.00

Cowboy

Cowboy Wristwatch
Date: 1970s • Maker: China
Animated gun. Cowboy dressed in red and blue.
$75.00 – 95.00

Davy Crockett

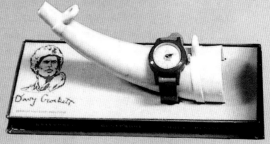

Davy Crockett Wristwatch
Date: 1954 • Maker: U.S. Time
Variation 1. Smaller sized powder horn. Sounds like a
kazoo when blown into. Watch case has green plastic
bezel. Decorative box lid showing Davy at the Alamo.
Watch only $125.00 – 175.00
Box and powder horn only $250.00 – 375.00

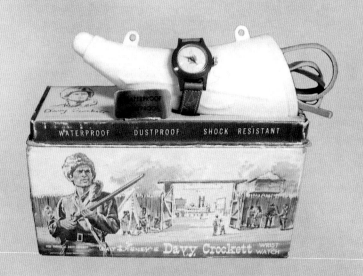

Davy Crockett Wristwatch
Date: 1954 • Maker: U.S. Time
Variation 2. Larger powder horn with rawhide strap.
Green plastic bezel. Watch displayed on powder horn.
Watch only $125.00 – 175.00
Box and powder horn only $250.00 – 375.00

Davy Crockett Wristwatch
Date: 1954 • Maker: U.S. Time
Variation 3. Close-up of Davy with chromium case.
$125.00 – 175.00

Davy Crockett Wristwatch
Date: 1954 • Maker: Muros Watch Factory
Animated gun at 6:00 position. Dial shows
Davy wearing coonskin cap and buckskin
jacket. Smaller sized gold-toned case.
$225.00 – 325.00

Davy Crockett Wristwatch
Date: 1956 • Maker: Bradley
Davy Crockett shown as 3D figure in front of western
background. Watch displayed in bottom of box.
Watch only $75.00 – 150.00
Scarce box only $375.00 – 475.00

Davy Crockett Wristwatch
Date: 1956 • Maker: Bradley
Close-up of colorful yellow and
blue dial with Davy holding rifle.
$75.00 – 150.00

Davy Crockett Wristwatch
Date: 1950s • Maker: Unknown
Dial shows Davy holding rifle. Smaller size with glow-in-
the-dark hands and numbers. Sweep red second hand.
$125.00 – 175.00

Davy Crockett Pendulette Clock
Date: 1955 • Maker: Unknown
Scarce. Colorful pendulette weight driven
wall clock. Davy shown in hunting position
with rifle. Round pendulum has picture of
Davy on it. Clock case made of masonite.
$300.00 – 400.00

Davy Crockett Clock Box
Date: 1955 • Maker: Unknown
Box shows picture of clock face.
$50.00 – 75.00

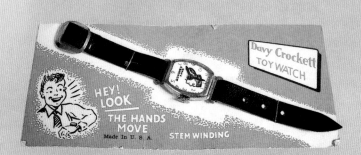

Davy Crockett Toy Watch
Date: 1950s • Maker: Unknown
Make-believe toy watch on header. Has picture of Davy
with red numbers. Black plastic watchband.
$50.00 – 75.00

Davy Crockett Pin-back
Date: 1950s • Maker: Premium
Pin-back shows Davy Crockett in hunting position. Color-
ful red and yellow "Sunbeam Bread" premium button.
$20.00 – 35.00

Gene Autry

Gene Autry Wristwatch
Date: 1948 • Maker: Wilane
Rectangular chromium case. Gene Autry riding his horse
Champion on dial. First Gene Autry wristwatch. Written
on back of case "Always Your Pal Gene Autry."
$250.00 – 400.00

Gene Autry Wristwatch
Date: 1948 • Maker: Wilane
Round chromium watch attached to stand-up insert.
Box lid has sketch of Gene Autry and horseshoe with
"Champion" printed on it. Western wristband and buckle.
Watch only $250.00 – 350.00
Box and insert only $275.00 – 375.00

Gene Autry Wristwatch
Date: 1948 • Maker: Wilane
Close-up of Gene on dial with white sweep second
hand. Glow-in-the-dark hands and numbers.
$250.00 – 350.00

Gene Autry Wristwatch
Date: 1951 • Maker: New Haven
Animated six-shooter gun between 6:00 and 7:00 posi-
tion. Western style wristband and buckle. Part of a series
that included Annie Oakley, Dick Tracy, Gene Autry, Li'l
Abner, and Texas Ranger.
$350.00 – 450.00

Hopalong Cassidy

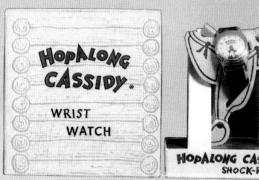

Hopalong Cassidy Wristwatch
Date: 1950 • Maker: U.S. Time
Metal watch displayed on saddle inside box.
Watch only $125.00 – 250.00
Box only $200.00 – 275.00

Hopalong Cassidy Wristwatch
Date: 1950 • Maker: U.S. Time
Close-up of Hoppy with red hands and numbers.
Western style wristband and buckle.
$125.00 – 200.00

Hopalong Cassidy Wristwatch
Date: 1950 • Maker: U.S. Time
Top portion of expansion band has brown
leatherette with alligator finish. Displayed on saddle.
Watch only $200.00 – 300.00
Box only $200.00 – 275.00

Hopalong Cassidy Wristwatch
Date: 1950 • Maker: U.S. Time
Variation 1. Small round chromium case. Western wrist-
band and buckle. Box lid shows Hoppy with hands on
hips. On insert Hoppy is pictured with his horse, Topper.
Watch only $125.00 – 200.00
Box only $370.00 – 575.00

Hopalong Cassidy Wristwatch
Date: 1960 • Maker: Great Britain
Hoppy's collar is less pointed
than the American version.
$175.00 – 250.00

Hopalong Cassidy Wristwatch
Date: 1950 • Maker: U.S. Time
Variation 2. Large chromium case and dial.
$150.00 – 225.00

Hopalong Cassidy Pocket Watch
Date: 1960 • Maker: Great Britain
Scarce. English version with greenish dial.
Collar is less pointed than American version.
$300.00 – 400.00

Hopalong Cassidy Pocket Watch
Date: 1955 • Maker: U.S. Time
Scarce. Black enameled case with small dial
showing Hoppy on obverse. Leather strap
with leather button attached to pocket watch.
Could be used as a lapel watch.
Pocket watch only $350.00 – 450.00
Leather fob only $60.00 – 90.00

Jeff Arnold

Hopalong Cassidy Pocket Watch
Date: 1955 • Maker: U.S. Time
Scarce. Reverse of pocket or
lapel watch is black enamel.
Pocket watch only $350.00 – 450.00
Leather fob only $60.00 – 90.00

Jeff Arnold Pocket Watch
Date: 1953 • Maker: Ingersoll L.T.D. (Great Britain)
Variation 1. Jeff Arnold with animated gun in left hand
at 4:00 position. Older man resembling Gabby Hayes
shown on obverse. England's version of Roy Rogers.
Glow-in-the-dark hands and numbers on dial.
$275.00 – 400.00

Jeff Arnold Pocket Watch
Date: 1953 • Maker: Ingersoll L.T.D. (Great Britain)
Variation 2. Between 11:00 and 1:00 position
Jeff Arnold is printed in black. Variation 1 has
Ingrersoll in the same position printed in black.
$275.00 – 400.00

Jeff Arnold Pocket Watch
Date: 1953 • Maker: Ingersoll L.T.D. (Great Britain)
Reverse of both Jeff Arnold pocket watches
show on eagle flying and the word "Eagle"
incised on back. This was probably a trademark
for Eagle Comic Books in England.
$275.00 – 400.00

Lone Ranger

Lone Ranger Wristwatch
Date: 1939 • Maker: New Haven
Large pre-war wristwatch. Lone Ranger riding Silver on
dial. Box and insert have same image. Western style
wristband and buckle.
Watch only $250.00 – 350.00
Box and insert only $275.00 – 475.00

Lone Ranger Wristwatch
Date: 1948 • Maker: New Haven
Rectangular case with picture of Lone Ranger riding
Silver. Reissue of 1939 watch. Fancy tooled leather
western wristband.
$200.00 – 300.00

Lone Ranger Wristwatch
Date: 1951 • Maker: New Haven (T.L.R. Inc.)
Round chromium dial with Lone
Ranger in red shirt riding Silver.
$150.00 – 225.00

Lone Ranger Pocket Watch Box
Date: 1940 • Maker: New Haven
Scarce. Red box for lapel or pocket watch.
Sketch of Silver and Lone Ranger on box lid.
Box only $200.00 – 225.00

Lone Ranger Pocket Watch
Date: 1940 • Maker: New Haven
Scarce. Close-up of black enamel obverse with small
center dial. Leather watch fob holster with miniature
gun. Printed on holster in white letters is "Lone Ranger."
Pocket watch only $275.00 – 475.00
Fob only $85.00 – 135.00

Lone Ranger Pocket Watch
Date: 1940 • Maker: New Haven
Scarce. Variation 1. Close-up of decal
on reverse. Yellow background with Silver
rearing up and cactus. Fob shown.
Pocket watch only $275.00 – 475.00
Fob only $85.00 – 125.00

Lone Ranger Pocket Watch
Date: 1940 • Maker: New Haven
Scarce. Variation 2. Nickel over brass case.
Decal shows Silver running. With white background.
Missing cactus. Printed words in different position.
$275.00 – 475.00

Lone Ranger Pin-Back
Date: 1938 • Maker: Unknown
Newspaper premium.
$35.00 – 55.00

Red Ryder

Ranger Pocket Watch
Date: 1930s • Maker: Smith's (Great Britain)
Animated cowboy at 4:00 position, riding the range.
$250.00 – 375.00

Red Ryder Wristwatch
Date: 1951 • Maker: Rexall Drug Co. (distributor)
Scarce. Paper face dial used over Bugs Bunny dial. Red
Ryder on black horse. Little Beaver in background.
$300.00 – 500.00

Roy Rogers Wristwatch
Date: 1951 • Maker: Ingraham
First Roy Rogers watch with Roy sitting on Trigger.
Rectangular case with expansion band. Cardboard
wood-grained box showing Roy and Trigger.
Watch only $175.00 – 275.00
Box only $250.00 – 350.00

Roy Rogers Wristwatch
Date: 1951 • Maker: Ingraham
Close-up of Roy on rearing Trigger. Expansion band.
$175.00 – 275.00

Roy Rogers Wristwatch
Date: 1950s • Maker: Ingraham
Roy and a rearing Trigger. Small rectangular
case. Western style wristband and buckle.
Red and yellow insert with clear plastic lid.
Watch only $175.00 – 275.00
Box and insert only $200.00 – 300.00

Roy Rogers Wristwatch
Date: 1950s • Maker: Ingraham
Close-up of smaller rectangular
chromium case with Roy and Trigger.
$175.00 – 275.00

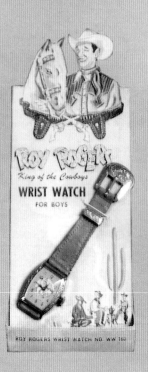

Roy Rogers Wristwatch
Date: 1951 • Maker: Ingraham
Head shot of Roy and Trigger posing.
Greenish dial with western style band.
Horizontal wood-grained cardboard box.
Watch only $200.00 – 300.00
Box only $175.00 – 275.00

Roy Rogers Wristwatch
Date: 1951 • Maker: Ingraham
Head shot of Roy and Trigger posing. Rectangular
chromium case. Western style wristband and buckle.
Attractive insert which can be used as easel.
Watch only $200.00 – 300.00
Box and insert only $200.00 – 300.00

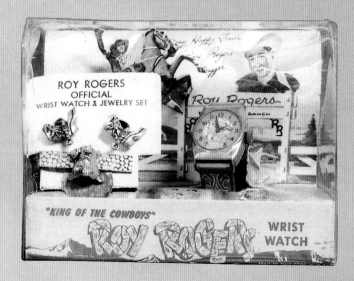

Roy Rogers Wristwatch
Date: 1956 • Maker: Bradley
Round gold-toned case. Roy and Trigger posing
on dial. Attractive dioramic western landscape
with Roy and Trigger in 3-D. Display box has
plastic slip cover. Gold-toned cuff link boots
and tie clasp saddle included in 3-D box.
Watch only $200.00 – 300.00
3-D box only $250.00 – 350.00
Jewelry $40.00 – 85.00

Roy Rogers Wristwatch
Date: 1956 • Maker: Bradley
Close-up of round gold-toned case
with Roy and Trigger posing.
$200.00 – 300.00

OFFICIAL WRIST WATCH and JEWELRY SET

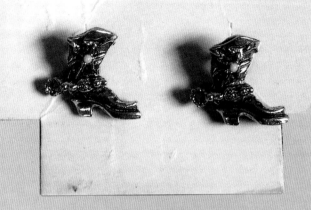

Roy Rogers Jewelry
Date: 1956 • Maker: Bradley
Carded jewelry set of chromium western boots used as cuff links. Accented by turquoise.
$25.00 – 40.00

Roy Rogers Reflector Strip
Date: 1960 • Maker: Ingraham
Scarce. Each strip has seven identical characters. Trigger rearing up as Roy waves. Reflector strips act as early hologram. Used on Ingraham wristwatch. Strips made for Roy Rogers, Dale Evans, majorette, and ballerina.
$100.00 – 175.00

Roy Rogers Pocket Watch
Date: 1959 • Maker: Bradley
Pocket watch with stopwatch feature. Roy pictured twice on dial. Chromium case. Colorful box lid showing enlarged picture of Roy and Trigger. Instruction tag included in box.
Pocket watch only $400.00 – 500.00
Box only $200.00 – 300.00

Roy Rogers Pin-Back
Date: 1950s • Maker: Unknown
Large pin-back showing portrait of Roy Rogers.
$20.00 – 35.00

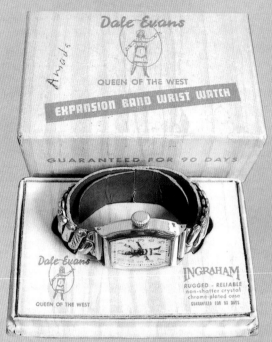

Dale Evans Wristwatch
Date: 1949 • Maker: Ingraham
Scarce. First Dale Evans wristwatch. Dale standing
in full costume on painted tin face. Rectangular
chromium case. Western style wristband and buckle.
$300.00 – 400.00

Dale Evans Wristwatch
Date: 1951 • Maker: Ingraham
Dale standing on watch dial with
expansion band. Wood-grained cardboard
box. Dale pictured with lariat on box lid.
Watch only $175.00 – 275.00
Box only $250.00 – 350.00

Dale Evans Wristwatch
Date: 1951 • Maker: Ingraham
Close-up of rectangular chromium case
with red numerals instead of brown as
with 1949 model. Expansion band.
$175.00 – 275.00

Dale Evans Wristwatch
Date: 1951 • Maker: Ingraham
Head shot of Dale and her horse, Buttermilk.
Rectangular chromium case with western-style band
and buckle. Attractive insert can be used as easel.
Watch only $200.00 – 300.00
Box and insert only $200.00 – 300.00

Dale Evans Wristwatch
Date: 1956 • Maker: Bradley
Rectangular chromium case. Dale and Buttermilk
posing in horseshoe on dial. Dioramic western
landscape with Dale on Buttermilk in 3-D display.
Box has plastic slip cover. Gold-toned
horseshoe necklace included in 3-D box.
Watch only $200.00 – 300.00
3-D box only $250.00 – 350.00
Jewelry $40.00 – 65.00

Dale Evans Wristwatch
Date: 1956 • Maker: Bradley
Rectangular gold-toned bezel with Dale
and Buttermilk posing in horseshoe on
dial. Western style wristband and buckle.
$250.00 – 350.00

Dale Evans Wristwatch
Date: 1951 • Maker: Ingraham
Variation 1. Dale and Buttermilk posing
in horseshoe with white background.
Round chromium case. Expansion band.
$125.00 – 175.00

Dale Evans Wristwatch
Date: 1955 • Maker: Ingraham
Variation 2. Brown background instead of white.
Dale and Buttermilk in horseshoe. Expansion band.
$125.00 – 175.00

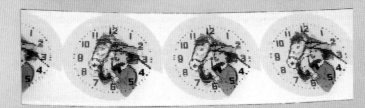

Dale Evans Reflector Strips
Date: 1960 • Maker: Ingraham
Scarce. Illusion of Dale and Buttermilk moving their heads. Act as early hologram when used on watch dial. Seven identical characters on strip. Other strips made include Roy Rogers, majorette, and ballerina.
$100.00 – 175.00

Texas Ranger Wristwatch
Date: 1950 • Maker: Muros Watch Factory
Scarce. Variation 1. Animated gun at 6:00 position. Round chromium case. Glow-in-the-dark hands and numerals. Annie Oakley and Paul Bunyon also made by Muros Watch Factory.
$200.00 – 300.00

Zorro

Texas Ranger Wristwatch
Date: 1950 • Maker: Muros Watch Factory
Scarce. Variation 2. Larger dial version.
$200.00 – 300.00

Zorro Wristwatch
Date: 1950 • Maker: Ingersoll/U.S. Time
Round chromium case with Zorro printed dial. Black felt hat acts as insert. Red box lid shows Zorro riding horse.
Watch only $85.00 – 125.00
Box and hat only $275.00 – 375.00

Category 15
Miscellaneous

Buster Brown Advertising Sign
Date: 1920s • Maker: Unknown
Advertising sign showing Tige and Buster
Brown pulling on a stocking. Stiff cardboard
with easel stand. Eight products listed on sign.
$75.00 – 125.00

Ingersoll Display Sign
Date: 1930s • Maker: Ingersoll
Colorful display sign. "Aero wrist" watches
advertised on sign. Easel back.
$75.00 – 125.00

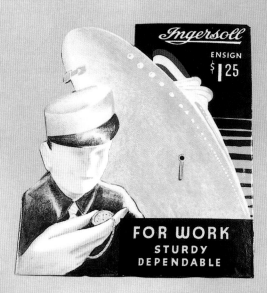

Ingersoll Display Sign
Date: 1930s • Maker: Ingersoll
Colorful display sign advertising "Ensign"
pocket watches. An ensign in the Navy is
shown with pocket watch. Easel back.
$75.00 – 125.00

Ingersoll Display Sign and Watch Box
Date: 1930s • Maker: Ingersoll
Jeweled "Rist-Arch" watch advertised on sign.
Curved watch box used with display sign. Sign
reads "Case Curved to Fit the Wrist." Easel back.
Sign only $65.00 –100.00
Box only $40.00 – 65.00

Ingersoll Display Sign
Date: 1930s • Maker: Ingersoll
"Swagger" wristwatch display sign. Easel back.
$40.00 – 75.00

Ingersoll Display Sign
Date: 1930s • Maker: Ingersoll
"Day-Break" wristwatch advertised on sign. Easel back.
$40.00 – 75.00

Ingersoll Display Sign
Date: 1930s • Maker: Ingersoll
"Call" wristwatch advertised on sign. Easel back.
$40.00 – 75.00

Ingersoll Window Display Sign
Date: 1930s • Maker: Ingersoll
Scarce. Tin display sign with two suction cups on front.
$125.00 – 200.00

Ingersoll Advertisement
Date: c. 1900 • Maker: Ingersoll
Cosmopolitan ad for a pocket watch commemorating
Admiral Dewey and other notables of the Spanish-
American War. Rare elegant pocket watch by Ingersoll.
Ad only $20.00 – 40.00

Ingersoll Advertisement
Date: 1930s • Maker: Ingersoll
Ingersoll Boy Scout watch ad for "Wrist Radiolite"
and "Yankee" pocket watch. Very suitable for scouting.
$20.00 – 40.00

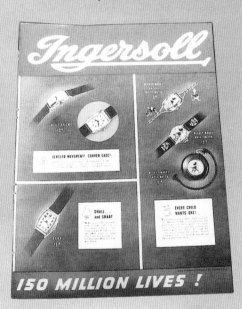

Ingersoll Advertisement
Date: 1937 • Maker: Ingersoll
Life magazine ad for Christmas of 1937.
Shows Mickey Mouse lapel watch, wristwatch
with three animated Mickey images and deluxe
watch with one animated Mickey at 6:00 position.
$40.00 – 60.00

Ingersoll Advertisement
Date: 1948 • Maker: Ingersoll
Ad appeared for Christmas 1948 showing
the 1947 Mickey Mouse wristwatch and the
new 1949 Bakelite Mickey Alarm Clock.
$15.00 – 30.00

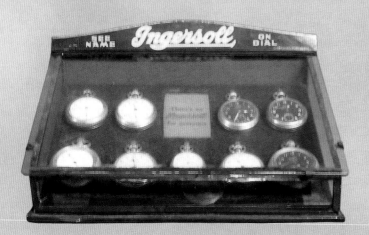

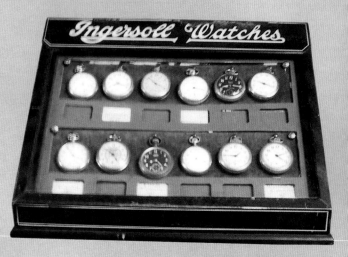

Ingersoll Display Case
Date: 1920s • Maker: Ingersoll
Display case holds nine different pocket watches.
Storage compartment in back of tin and glass case.
Case only $100.00 – 200.00

Ingersoll Display Case
Date: 1920s • Maker: Ingersoll
Display case holds 12 different pocket watches
with storage compartment in back. Tin and glass case.
Case only $100.00 – 200.00

Ingersoll Display Case
Date: 1920s • Maker: Ingersoll
Tin and glass case. Ideal for
displaying five alarm clocks.
Case only $150.00 – 250.00

Ingersoll Display Case
Date: 1930s • Maker: Ingersoll
Vertical wooden deluxe display case.
Velvet background. Ideal for displaying 12
pocket watches. Storage in back.
Case only $200.00 – 300.00

Kelton Display Case
Date: 1940s • Maker: Kelton
Oval glass window framed by leatherette border.
Velvet background. Used to display Kelton watches.
Case only $100.00 – 200.00

New Haven Display Case
Date: 1920s • Maker: New Haven
Slanted tin and glass case. Displays six
pocket watches and one wristwatch.
Storage compartment in back of case.
Case only $100.00 – 200.00

New Haven Character Watch Display
Date: 1951 • Maker: New Haven
Rare. N.O.S. (new old stock). Features three animated
Li'l Abner and three animated Dick Tracy watches. Each
watch cost $6.95. Some displays featured animated
Gene Autry and animated Annie Oakley watches.
$2,200.00 – 3,600.00

Watch Crystal Display Sign
Date: 1920s • Maker: Unknown
Art Deco sign depicts three "Sha-Ta-Pruf"
crystals that can replace older crystals.
$100.00 – 175.00

New Additions

1904 Pocket Watch Fob
Date: 1904 • Maker: Unknown
"St. Louis"/"1904"/"Louisiana Purchase 1803" embossed
on obverse. Fairgrounds of exposition also embossed
on center of fob. Commemorates Anniversary of the
Louisiana Purchase.
$75.00 – 100.00

Admiral Byrd Fob
Date: c. 1928 • Maker: Ingraham
Scarce. Trailblazer commemorative pocket watch fob.
Obverse shows Admiral Byrd's plane flying over Antarc-
tica. "Wings Over the Pole" embossed on obverse. Two
penguins and compass adorn the obverse.
$135.00 – 200.00

Admiral Dewey Pocket Watch
Date: 1900 • Maker: Ingersoll
Rare. Colorful pocket watch with portraits of President
William McKinley at 12:00 position. Other Spanish Ameri-
can War notables include General Nelson Miles, General
William Shafter, Admiral William Sampson, and at 6:00
position Colonel Theodore Roosevelt. Commodore
George Dewey in center of dial.
$700.00 – 1,200.00

Admiral Dewey Pocket Watch
Date: 1900 • Maker: Ingersoll
Rare. Reverse of pocket watch has
engraving of flagship Olympia. "Dewey"
and "Olympia" engraved on back as well.
$700.00 – 1,200.00

Alice In Wonderland Clock
Date: 1930s • Maker: Unknown
Scarce. Mad Hatter animated at 7:00 position.
Comic character looking sketch of Alice. "Alice" printed
on dial at 10:00 position. Aqua painted wooden case.
$175.00 – 275.00

A.O.A Wristwatch
Date: c. 1960 • Maker: Hamilton
"America Ordnance Association" in black on
gold-toned eagle and shield. Silver-toned background
on dial with gold-tone numbers, hands, and sweep sec-
ond hand. Vantage model. Possibly related to
Civil Defense. "To Provide for the Common
Defense"/"A.O.A." printed in gold on black bezel.
$85.00 – 150.00

Brownie Scout Wristwatch
Date: 1937 • Maker: New Haven
Scarce. Satin finish dial with chromium link band. Brown
numerals with "New Haven" printed under 12:00 posi-
tion. Box reads "Brownie Wrist Watch" on lid. Sears,
Roebuck and Co. guarantee slip included in box.
Watch only $125.00 – 225.00
Box only $125.00 – 225.00

Capitol Pocket Watch
Date: c.1940s • Maker: Ingraham
Scarce. Sketch of U.S. Capitol building on obverse.
Greenish dial with second hands, fancy case.
$150.00 – 225.00

Davy Crockett Wristwatch
Date: 1954 • Maker: Liberty
Scarce. "Davy Crockett" name stamped in red on dial.
Small red flintlock pistol pictured at 7:00 position.
$125.00 – 175.00

Flash Gordon Wristwatch
Date: 1979 • Maker: Bradley
Full figure of Flash Gordon shooting his
ray gun. Futuristic city in background. Plastic
case with cardboard sleeve. "By Bradley"
imprinted in gold on cream base.
Watch only $90.00 – 125.00
Box with sleeve only $30.00 – 60.00

Girl Scout Wristwatch
Date: 1932 • Maker: Ingersoll
Scarce. Girl Scout emblem on center of dial.
Gold colored numbers on silvery face. Seven
jewels in chromium case. Early expansion band.
$275.00 – 375.00

Ingersoll Aero Wristwatch Box
Date: 1940s • Maker: Ingersoll
Box attachment that was part of Ingersoll
Aero Wristwatch display. Silver colored box
with navy blue plane pictured on it.
$60.00 – 75.00

Louie The Duck Wristwatch
Date: 1947 • Maker: Ingersoll
Rare. Showing nephew of Donald
Duck. Part of 1947 series which
included Danny the Black Lamb,
Fiddler Pig, and Snow White.
$300.00 – 475.00

Mickey Mouse and Pluto Fob
Date: 1933 • Maker: Ingersoll
Rare. Mickey hunting with Pluto on
brass enameled fob. Uncommon
variation.
$225.00 – 325.00

Storm Clock
Date: 1933 • Maker: United
Scarce. Double animation clock
showing helmsman moving ship's
wheel on dial. Decorative metal
case showing large figure of helmsman at wheel.
$250.00 – 350.00

Mickey Mouse Pocket Watch Fob
Date: 1934 • Maker: Ingersoll Ltd. (Great Britain)
Rare. Mickey Mouse fob used with English
pocket watch. Red, white, and black colors
distinguish Mickey on obverse.
$175.00 – 275.00

Mickey Mouse Pocket Watch Fob
Date: 1934 • Maker: Ingersoll Ltd. (Great Britain)
Rare. Engraved on reverse of English
fob "Ingersoll"/"Mickey Mouse"/"Watches
and Clocks"/"Copyright Walt Disney."
$175.00 – 275.00

Toppie Pocket Watch
Date: 1950s • Maker: Columbia Time Products
Pink checkered elephant "Toppie" pictured
on dial. Possibly a premium pocket watch for
Tip-Top Bread. Toppie's name on black blanket.
"Top Value Enterprises Inc." printed on edge of dial.
$95.00 – 150.00

Water Wheel Clock
Date: 1920s • Maker: Lux Clock Mfg. Co.
Scarce. Animated water wheel on old mill. Waterfall
and cottage depict a rural landscape. Paper dial with
green numbers. Decorative octagonal gold-toned case.
Green enamel leaves and filigree adorn bezel.
$175.00 – 300.00

World's Fair Pocket Watch
Date: 1964 • Maker: Unknown
Small pocket watch commemorating 1964 – 1965
New York World's Fair. Kaleidoscopic feature in center
of dial in black and gold on obverse. Gold-toned
numbers, hands, and case. Blue and red background.
$95.00 – 135.00

World's Fair Pocket Watch
Date: 1964 • Maker: Unknown
"N.Y. World's Fair" and "1964/1965" engraved on reverse.
Gold-toned globe shown on blue and red background.
$95.00 – 135.00

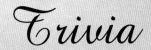

Trivia

Betty Boop Pocket Watch

The Betty Boop pocket watch made by Ingraham in 1934 has become extremely rare (less than 10 have shown up). The pocket watch became unpopular because young boys didn't identify with a female character. The parents also felt the pocket watch was too sexy and inappropriate. As a result very few have survived.

Buck Rogers Pocket Watch

The Buck Rogers pocket watch was produced by Ingraham in 1935. On the obverse the copper lightening bolt hands were made and filed by hand. Upon close examination one can see the rough file marks.

The engraved monster on the reverse has been called the Cyclops, one-eyed monster, and hairy monster. But according to old advertising he is called the Tiger Man. In 1935 the Buck Rogers pocket watch and decorative box sold for less than $1.00.

Clocks

Some late nineteenth century and early twentieth century clocks were made of brass and tin with nickel-plated cases. They also had long thin legs. This is why they became known as tin can or long-legged clocks.

Dick Tracy Wristwatch

In 1951 the New Haven Co. produced a Dick Tracy wristwatch. Instead of using an animated automatic-style gun they used an animated six-shooter, which was also used on their animated Gene Autry wristwatch. The animated automatic-style gun is harder to find than the western-style pistol. None pictured.

Flash Gordon Wristwatch

In 1971 the Precision Watch Co. made a limited number of Flash Gordon wristwatches (including a decorative box). The watch was produced jointly with a Japanese firm. Due to poor communication with the Japanese, who thought they were making a Mickey Mouse wristwatch, production was stopped. As a result less than 200 Flash Gordon wristwatches were produced. This is the only wristwatch Precision Time ever made.

Glow-in-the-dark Hands and Numbers

During the post war years (1946 – 1950) glow-in-the-dark hands and numbers were used on several timepieces. There were some articles written about the hazards of using glow-in-the-dark items. They warned that small amounts of radium could cause serious health problems. These claims were never really substantiated.

Kelton Mickey Mouse Wristwatch

The Kelton Co. made the first postwar Mickey Mouse wristwatch in 1946. During World War II there was an embargo or restriction on making metal timepieces. On the Kelton wristwatch, Mickey Mouse's head is on a tin post revolving with the hour hand. In 1947 Ingersoll resumed making other Disney wristwatches.

Mickey Mouse Wristwatch

The 1937 – 1938 Ingersoll Mickey Mouse wristwatch is sometimes called the Fred Astaire watch. On the lid Mickey is wearing a silk top hat and holding a cane. He looks happy and fancy-free. On the inside of the box lid, Mickey has his eyes closed and looks like he's had a night on the town.

Popeye Pocket Watch

The Popeye pocket watch was made in 1934 by the Ingraham Co. It has a very colorful dial with all the Thimble Theater Players on the dial. The company thought the dial was too busy and crowded. One year later they simplified the dial by using a large image of Popeye and eliminating all the Thimble Theater Players except the animated Wimpy. They made it easier to read the time.

Red Ryder Wristwatch

The Red Ryder wristwatch was produced in 1951 and distributed by the Rexall Drug Stores. For some reason the Red Ryder dial was pasted over the Bugs Bunny dial, which was produced in 1951 as well. Upon close examination the green foliage on the Bugs Bunny dial can be seen on the center portion of the Red Ryder dial.

Bibliography

A Celebration of Comic Art and Memorabilia
by Robert Lesser, 1975, Hawthorn Books

Comic Character Clocks and Watches
by Howard Brenner, 1981, Books Americana, Inc.

Comic Character Timepieces
by Hy Brown with Nancy Thomas, 1992, Schiffer Publishing, Ltd.

Complete Price Guide to Watches
by Richard E. Gilbert, Tom Engle, and Cooksey Shugart, 2009, Collector Books

Hakes' Price Guide to Character Toys
by House of Collectibles, 2004, Gemstone Publishing

Pastime
by Phillip Collins, 1993, Chronicle Books

Small Clock Tickertape
by Louise Dworatcheck, 2000, Dworatcheck and Dworatcheck

Vintage American and European Character Wristwatches Price Guide
by David A. Mycko and The Ehrhardts, 1989, Heart of America Press

Periodicals
Bulletin of the National Association of Watch and Clock Collectors (NAWCC) August 1967, Vol. XII, No. 11

Bulletin of the National Association of Watch and Clock Collectors (NAWCC) August 1974, Vol. XX, No. 4

Hobbies, The Magazine for Collectors January 1972, Lightner Publishing Corporation

Index

Index